129 BIRDS IN FULL COLOR

BIRDS

A GUIDE TO FAMILIAR AMERICAN BIRDS

by
HERBERT S. ZIM, Ph.D.
and
IRA N. GABRIELSON, LL.D., D. Sc.

Revised and Updated by
CHANDLER S. ROBBINS

Illustrated by
JAMES GORDON IRVING

GOLDEN PRESS • NEW YORK
Western Publishing Company, Inc.
Racine, Wisconsin

FOREWORD

This book pictures in full color 129 of the most familiar American birds. Using these birds as keys, the text describes additional related and similar species, helping the reader to identify more than 250 birds in all.

The selection of the most common birds of America and the assembling of concise information about them were achieved through long, detailed study of voluminous data on our bird life. This might have been an impossible task were it not for the wholehearted cooperation and assistance of ornithologists and other naturalists. John Aldrich, C. A. Cottam, Allen Duvall, D. F. Hoffmeister, A. C. Martin, Ernst Mayr, A. L. Nelson, A. Sprunt IV, R. E. Stewart, H. L. Webster, and Alex Wetmore gave helpful comments and suggestions. Special thanks are due to Chandler S. Robbins of the Patuxent Wildlife Research Center, who compiled the basic data for the range maps, and checked migration dates, tabular data, and other factual information. James Gordon Irving has contributed his knowledge of birds as well as his unusual artistic talent.

This Revised Edition, prepared by Chandler S. Robbins, includes the latest information about birds, as well as recent changes in scientific and common names, bird classification, and geographical distributions.

H.S.Z.
I.N.G.

Revised Edition, 1987

HOW TO USE THIS BOOK

This is a field book made to fit your pocket when you go looking for birds. Check each range map (example below) for birds that occur in your region. Concentrate on these birds. Areas where birds live in summer are shown in red; winter areas are in blue. Purple shows areas where the bird is a permanent resident.

Migrating birds pass over parts of the white areas in spring and fall. Check their "timetable" as given on pp. 132-153, where you will also find information on nests, eggs, and food. Mark each bird you are likely to see, and when you have seen it, record the date and place. Thumb through this book and become familiar with the birds. Then, when you see them, you'll recognize some at first sight. Also use the information on pp. 154-155 concerning books, museums, and places to see birds.

The more you look at this book, the more facts you'll find. The color plates show spring plumage of adult male birds, and usually females or young if they are very different. The text emphasizes size, field marks, important facts, differences between males and females, and related birds that are similar. The birds have been selected so that knowing one bird will help you to know others like it.

The birds illustrated are among the most common and the ones you have the best chance of seeing. No rare birds are pictured. In almost every part of the United States and southern Canada you can see many of the birds in this book—plus other common local birds you will soon learn to know.

HOW TO IDENTIFY BIRDS

Most birds can be identified at a glance by experts because they know exactly what to look for. With practice you too can become an expert.

Whereas some wildflower guides are arranged by color, bird guides are generally organized so that closely related species—those of similar shape and behavior—are together. Water birds appear first, followed by the more primitive land birds; the true songbirds are last.

One quickly learns to sort unknown birds into the major categories called orders, such as herons, ducks, hawks, kingfishers, woodpeckers, and perching birds (see pages 9-11). For water birds, note whether they wade, swim, or dive; for aerial feeders whether they constantly flap, soar, or hover. For all birds, look closely at the size and shape of the bill (pages 14-15) and the shape and length of the tail. Compare the total length with that of some familiar species. Is it the size of a kinglet, a warbler, a sparrow, an oriole, a robin, a flicker, or a crow? These characters will help place birds in the correct family.

The next step is to determine the species by looking for the presence or absence of wing bars, tail patterns, eye rings or eye stripes, and color patterns on the head and elsewhere. Is the back plain or streaked? Do the underparts have horizontal bars or longitudinal streaks? Eye color is important for owls and some vireos.

Behavior can also provide valuable clues. Does the bird walk or hop or run? Does it wag its tail? Does it catch insects on the wing and eat in flight like a swift or swallow? Or does it repeatedly return to an exposed perch to eat insect prey like a flycatcher or waxwing? Does it climb up a tree trunk like a woodpecker or a Brown Creeper, or work head-down like a nuthatch? Does it eat berries like a thrush or an oriole, or probe in the ground for worms and grubs like a robin, blackbird, or starling? See pages 132-153 for the principal foods of each species.

EQUIPMENT The only essential equipment for seeing birds is a pair of eyes. Good ears are a help, too. But there are ways of increasing your enjoyment, none of which involves much expense. This book is one, for a guide book is important. As you acquire experience, you will want more advanced books (see page 154). Your own records, if kept systematically, are an important part of your equipment. A pocket notebook to record detailed information is worth carrying. Rugged clothing, waterproof boots, and a bottle of mosquito repellent are part of an experienced birder's equipment.

Field glasses or binoculars are the most important and most expensive item of equipment. There's no denying their value in bringing tree-top birds down to you. Like a good camera, a good pair of binoculars is a precision tool and should be selected with care. The best glasses are made with prisms to reduce their size. The power of the glass tells how much closer it makes a bird appear. Through 6x (6-power) glasses a bird looks six times as close. Glasses of 6x to 8x are best. Remember, the higher the power, the more limited your field of vision. Glasses that admit the most light are the best. This depends on the width of the front lens (usually measured in millimeters). A 6 x 35 lens admits twice as much light as a 6 x 24. The large 7 x 50 binoculars are excellent for birds. Those that adjust by a single center focusing screw are most convenient.

WHERE TO LOOK Birds are everywhere, but to see the most birds try looking in the best places: in moist woodlands or perhaps at the edge of a wooded swamp. Young scrubby woods are likely to have more birds than mature forests. Wood margins are generally good, especially during migration. But no single place is best. Saltwater marshes and shores will yield birds that one will never find in pine woods. Other species prefer open fields, or western deserts. A wooded park in the midst of a city is one of the very best places to look for birds during migrations. If you explore your own region, you will discover certain spots are favored—perhaps a small glen with a brook, a wooded point on a lake, a marsh, or cottonwoods along a river. On page 155 is a list of some famous places to see birds. Make local inquiries. See also the books and museums listed on page 154.

HOW TO LOOK Experienced watchers go out early in the morning when birds are most active, and will often sit quietly in a likely spot and let the birds come to them. Keen-eyed birds are easily frightened by movement. Don't make yourself conspicuous against the open sky. Move slowly. Try to cover several distinct habitats, if possible—a woodland, marsh, field, river bank, shore, or whatever your locality affords. Eventually you will work out a route that will give you the greatest variety of birds per time spent. Experience in your own region will be your best help. Make bird watching a year-round activity, for each season has its own special surprises and delights to offer the careful observer.

WHY LOOK? Birding is enjoyed by millions of North Americans of all ages, and by millions of others all over the world. It is a hobby that can give pleasure at any place and at any time. Some prefer to do their observing by themselves, others prefer the sociability of birding as a small group. There are more than 700 bird clubs in the United States and well over 100 in Canada.

Birds are by far the most popular of wildlife because they are easy to see, easy to identify, great in numbers and variety, beautiful to observe, attractive to hear, and ever changing in occurrence and numbers. Even the experts get many thrills from finding unusual or unexpected species. Many species migrate long distances, and at times large numbers of birds are blown off course and are discovered hundreds of miles from their usual homes. A few western birds even occur on the Atlantic coast and vice versa.

Many birders enjoy competition, such as beating the previous year's bird list, finding more species than a friend, or being the first to spot a returning migrant. Thousands of people take bird tours to exotic places. Many others keep impressive lists of the species they have discovered right at home. Bird feeders and bird baths also bring much pleasure to shut-ins.

An interest in birds often expands into a greater appreciation for all wildlife, and for the habitats that are essential to their survival. Many birders develop into wildlife photographers or leaders of scouting or other youth groups. In any case, one acquires an absorbing hobby that can be enjoyed throughout life.

PARTS OF A BIRD

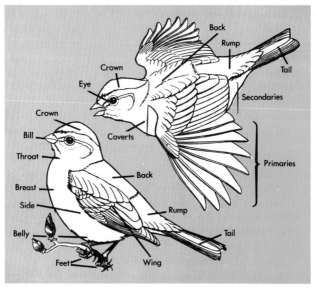

Names are tools. Bird experts have dozens of technical names for the various parts of birds. Using these terms, they can describe a bird with great accuracy. The beginner does not have the experience to use these terms, so only the essential technical terms are used in this book. When you see a bird you cannot identify and want help from an expert, try to observe the bird so well that you can describe its size, habits, and the color and form of the parts illustrated above. Put your information down on paper (don't trust your memory). By keeping these few parts in mind you will systematize your observations and record the details needed to get your bird identified.

BIRD CLASSIFICATION

Birds are grouped into orders, families, and genera according to similarities of bills, feet, and internal anatomy. If you know these groups, the relationship and classification of birds will be clearer. Here is a simplified list of the main bird groups in this book; a family tree (pages 12-13) shows their relationships. On pages 156-157 are listed the scientific names of all the birds illustrated. These names and the English names used are those adopted by the A.O.U. (American Ornithologists' Union) Committee on Classification and Nomenclature.

LOONS: Large swimming and diving birds; tails short; legs set far back. Four toes: 3 front ones fully webbed. Bill sharply pointed, higher than wide. **page 21**

GREBES: Smaller swimmers and divers. Tail lacking; legs far back. Four toes with thin skin flaps (lobes) and with flattened nails. Bill slender, pointed; higher than wide. **page 22**

HERONS and BITTERNS: Long-legged wading birds. In flight, feet extend beyond tail but neck is pulled in. Bill straight and sharp; skin between eye and bill bare. Four toes, scarcely webbed or not webbed at all. Middle toenail has comblike margin. **pages 23-25**

DUCKS, GEESE, and SWANS: Swimming birds with distinct tails. Legs centered. Birds walk well compared to grebes and loons. Four toes, front 3 webbed. Bill broad and flat, often with "teeth" along edge. Upper bill ending in short, flat hook or "nail." **pages 26-33**

CRANES, RAILS, and COOTS: Marsh birds flying with neck extended and feet dangling (rails); wings rounded. Four toes, unwebbed (except for coot, which has lobes). Middle toenail without comblike margin (see Herons). Feathered between eye and bill. **page 34**

PLOVERS, SANDPIPERS, and SNIPES: Long-legged shorebirds, mostly small. Bill usually conical, long and soft; nostrils opening through slits in bill. Generally 4 toes: hind toe raised and short. Sanderlings and most plovers have only 3 toes.

pages 35-39

GULLS and TERNS: Mostly light-colored marine birds. Wings long, narrow and pointed. Bill hooked (gulls) or pointed (terns) with nostrils opening into slits that go through bill. Four toes: hind toe small and not webbed.

pages 40-41

HAWKS, EAGLES, and VULTURES: Large birds. Bill strongly hooked; feet powerful, claws long and curved. Vultures differ in having a bare head with nostrils connected by hole through bill. **pages 42-47**

GROUSE, QUAIL, and TURKEY: Land birds that scratch for food. Bills short and stout. Feet heavy, strong; hind toe short and raised. Wings short and rounded.

pages 48-50

PIGEONS and DOVES: Small-headed birds with slender bills, grooved at base; and with nostrils opening through a bare fleshy area at base of bill. Legs short. Four toes, all on same level. Hind toe as long as shortest front one. **pages 51-52**

CUCKOOS: Long, slim birds with slightly curved bill. Tail long, feathers not stiff or pointed; central tail feathers longest. Four toes: 2 in front; 2 behind. **page 53**

OWLS: Bills strongly hooked. Toes with large curved claws; entire leg feathered. Eyes large and immovable in puffy, feathered "face." **pages 54-56**

SWIFTS: Small swallowlike birds; bill small with no bristles at base. Mouth wide. Wings slender and very long, reaching beyond tail; tail with 10 feathers. **page 57**

GOATSUCKERS: Birds with large heads, small bills, and wide mouths. Bill usually with bristles at base. Feet small; middle toe long with comblike claw. Feathers soft, dull-colored. **pages 58-59**

HUMMINGBIRDS: Tiny birds with bill slender and needlelike—longer than head. Feet small, weak. Feathers on back usually shiny green. **page 60**

KINGFISHERS: Head large and crested. Bill long, strong, pointed. Feet small and weak. Four toes: 2 of the 3 forward toes joined for half their length. **page 61**

WOODPECKERS: Climbing birds. Bill strong, pointed, with bristles at nostril. Tail feathers stiff and pointed. Toes: 2 in front, 2 in back; or (rarely) 2 in front and 1 in back. **pages 62-65**

PERCHING BIRDS: The largest bird group. Land birds, mostly small, with 4 toes—all on the same level, never webbed. Hind toe as long as middle front toe—an adaptation for perching. Tail with 12 feathers. **pages 66-127**

Vultures

Pelicans

Loons

Petrels and Kin

Storks

Flamingo

Ibis

Herons

Boobies

Anhinga

Nuthatches

Cormorants

Tropicbirds

Falcons

Gulls and Terns

Grebes

Plovers

Sandpipers

Jacana

Cranes

Limpkin

Coots and Rails

Pigeons

Quails and Kin

Waterfowl

Parrots

A FAMILY TREE OF BIRDS

The 860 species of birds in North America north of Mexico are classified into 70 families. The major families and their approximate relationships are shown here. Families with the most species north of Mexico are represented by the thickest branches.

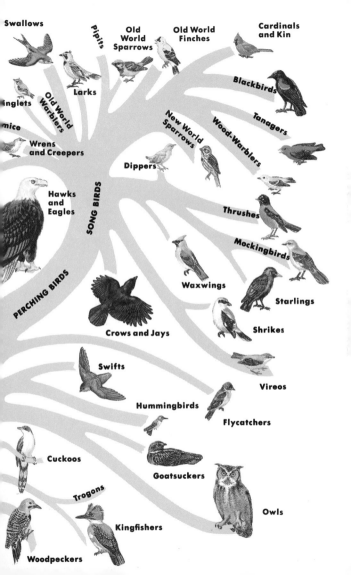

Tern   Loon   Heron   Kingfisher

ADAPTATIONS OF BIRDS

ADAPTATION

Birds show unusual adaptations to their way of life. The most important and obvious is a covering of feathers. These have developed from the scaly covering of reptiles. Each feather has rows of branched barbs that hook together. On the long flight feathers, the barbs mesh tightly to form a firm structure. Contour feathers and an undercoat of finer down cover the bird's body. Form and structure of feathers vary with different birds.

Internal adaptations of birds include air sacs and light, hollow bones; a very rapid heart; temperature several degrees higher than ours, and other structures favoring a very active existence. The animal food of birds includes insects, worms, mollusks, fish, and small mammals. Plant foods include seeds, buds, leaves, and fruits. Bills have obvious adaptations related to diet. Above are four birds, each from a different family, with similar bills adapted for eating fish.

Robin-perching

Ptarmigan-feathered

Pheasant-walking

Duck-swimming

Primary Flight Feather

Barbs and barbules enlarged

vane   shaft   quill

Shrike   Cardinal   Wood Thrush   Crossbill   Yellowthroat

OF FEET

Owl—
grasping

Woodpecker
—climbing

Yellowlegs
—wading

Coot—
swimming

Above are five birds all belonging to the same order, perching birds. Each of these species has developed a very different type of bill suited for eating particular foods. These are divergent developments from a common family ancestor. This type of development is also common.

Other adaptations are shown in the legs and feet of birds. The bird's three or four toes have been modified for climbing, scratching, grasping and tearing, and swimming. Long toes distribute the weight of birds that walk on mud and sand. Extra feathering protects the feet of ptarmigans and arctic owls. The long legs of waders, the webbed feet of swimmers, and other adaptations indicate specialized uses of various kinds.

Most interesting of all adaptations are those of behavior. Many species have developed distinct patterns of living. Careful observations will disclose the "personalities" of different birds and their social adaptations.

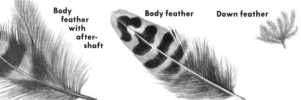

Body feather with aftershaft

Body feather

Down feather

Lewis' Woodpecker at feeding station

AMATEUR ACTIVITIES

Everyone starts watching birds with the same ideas in mind: to learn their names, to identify as many as possible, and to see what kind of "records" his watching will yield. Some people are content doing these things and never venture beyond this stage. Others find many more ways to broaden their knowledge. Time, place, and experience will determine how far you want to go. Here are some suggestions:

Downy Woodpeckers like suet

ATTRACTING BIRDS BY FEEDING

Birds were here long before people fed them—and they will continue to feed and care for themselves. But if severe cold or ice cuts off the food supply of winter birds, cooperative efforts are sometimes essential to save them. If you want to attract birds to your yard or window, then feeding them will help. Place feed on a platform or window shelf to retard spoiling and to provide some protection from predators. Find out how to build feeding stations. Set them near shrubbery to give the birds shelter. Place lumps of suet in wire containers for creepers, chickadees, nuthatches, and woodpeckers. Small grain (sunflower seeds, hemp, millet, and canary seed) will attract seed-eaters. At a window station you can watch birds feed.

Siskins and other finches enjoy sunflower and thistle seeds

ATTRACTING BIRDS BY WATERING

Birds need drinking and bathing water just as much as they need food. A watering place will attract birds during warm months when wild food is available. Birds like moving, shallow water. A dripping hose or a trickle of water running into a one-inch pan with gravel on the bottom is excellent. An old bucket with a triangular piece of cloth pulled through a drip hole and hung over an old baking pan will do as well as any elaborate cement pool.

Drip-bucket provides water

ATTRACTING BIRDS WITH COVER AND SHELTER

Birds need cover for protection against wind, cold, and enemies. The best kind of cover for birds is shrubs and vines that provide food as well as a place to hide. Plants that look attractive to us are not necessarily attractive to birds. Native plants that retain their fruit in winter are best. Nesting boxes are seldom satisfactory unless they are built with a specific bird in mind. A box for a wren must be very different from one for a flicker. Get complete instructions.

Martin box

Wren house

Wood Duck house

Build a box that can be easily cleaned and used year after year. Don't place boxes too close; three or four nesting boxes to an acre are usually enough. Most birds set up their own "territory" and will keep other birds out.

CREATING A LOCAL REFUGE   A group of people may find a way to create a local bird refuge to help birds care for themselves. Most communities have swamp or wasteland which can easily be developed into a bird refuge. Parks, golf courses, and cemeteries have been successful. Ample water supply is needed. Small dams across a brook will create shallow ponds that attract many birds. Swamp plants and grasses should be encouraged as seed producers. Evergreens may be planted for shelter.

BIRD PHOTOGRAPHY   Hunting with a gun is giving way to hunting with a camera. Only a few species of game birds may be shot, but you may photograph any bird. Bird photography offers thrills and hard work. It calls for patience and skill, but one fine shot makes it all worthwhile. Use a camera with a focal plane shutter and a fast lens. A flash bulb is usually necessary for close photos even in daylight, because many birds prefer to feed in the shade.

Steller's Jay (11 in.), only crested jay of the western conifers

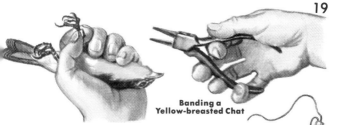

Banding a Yellow-breasted Chat

BIRD BANDING Thin aluminum bands are put around birds' legs to help in scientific studies. From the 43 million birds banded we have learned much about migrations, flyways, life spans, population changes, and annual returns to the same nesting or wintering areas.

Cooperation of thousands of amateurs has greatly assisted scientific study of birds. If you find a banded bird sick or dead (except a pigeon), look for a serial number, like "1240-24401" or "509-30091." An address either outside or inside the band may read "Avise Bird Band Write Wash DC USA". Write the number on a postcard, stating when, where, how, and by whom the bird was found. Send the card to the Bird Banding Laboratory, Patuxent Wildlife Research Center, Laurel, Md. 20708. They will send you the bird's history, and your report will help their studies.

Permits to band birds are issued to qualified persons involved in special studies. An applicant must be at least 18 years old, must describe the proposed research in detail, and must give names of three experts who will vouch for his or her qualifications.

Color bands

Official bird bands

BIRD COUNTS AND CENSUSES After you learn the common birds, you will begin to keep lists of the species you see. This is the beginning of an absorbing hobby. Soon your lists may include estimates of the number of birds seen as well as the species. Next you may do a complete census of a specific area that will show the density of the bird population there. Many bird clubs all over North America make one-day Christmas Bird Counts during Christmas season. To participate, contact a local bird club or write to *American Birds*, National Audubon Society, 950 Third Avenue, New York, N.Y. 10022. Counts made during the breeding season reveal from 2 to 20 adult birds per acre, depending on the type of vegetation (habitat) and the locality. Carefully made counts, especially those repeated year after year such as on a Breeding Bird Survey route, are of real scientific value. Special counts made during migrations, or counts of bird colonies or bird roosts, help us understand more about certain unusual species.

BREEDING BIRD ATLASES In many states and provinces, intensive mapping projects are in progress to show the nesting range of every bird species. Each state is divided into squares of about 10 square miles each, and volunteers compile nesting season lists of birds found in each square. Evidence of nesting, such as adults carrying nesting material or food for young makes the records especially valuable. These Atlas projects usually take five years to complete. Then they are repeated after a period of years to find out what changes in bird distribution have occurred. To find out whether an Atlas project is in progress in your area, contact the Laboratory of Ornithology, Cornell University, 159 Sapsucker Woods Road, Ithaca, N.Y. 14850.

COMMON LOON Spot loons by their large size, long body, short neck, pointed bill, and loud, yodel-like call. Loons are expert divers, but kick along the water before taking flight. In winter, Common Loon (24 in.) is gray above and white beneath. The slender-billed Red-throated Loon (17 in.) and Pacific Loon (18 in.) are recognized in summer by red or black throat patch contrasting with gray head.

PIED-BILLED GREBE Grebes are expert divers and swimmers. Smaller than most ducks, they float lower in the water, and are rarely seen in flight. The Pied-billed Grebe (9 in.) has a more rounded bill than other grebes. The throat patch is lacking in winter. The Horned Grebe

(9½ in.) is told in summer by black head with bright chestnut ear patches. Red-necked Grebe (13 in.) is grayer, with conspicuous white cheek patches and a long, pointed, yellowish bill.

GREAT BLUE HERON, our largest dark-colored wader, flies with a slow, regular wing beat. It usually nests in colonies. It gives a series of low-pitched croaks when flushed. Told from other herons by its size (38 in.). The slender-billed Tricolored Heron (22 in.) of southern coastal marshes has a sharply contrasting white belly. The medium-sized adult Black-crowned Night-Heron (21 in.) is black above, all-white beneath; young are heavily streaked brown and white.

GREEN-BACKED HERON This small solitary heron (14 in.) is scarcely larger than a crow. It has a typical heron flight, with slow, deep wing strokes. Like other herons it eats aquatic animals. At a distance it may be confused with the larger American Bittern (23 in.) or an immature night-heron (21 in.), but its body is unstreaked and its yellow-orange legs are distinctive. When alarmed it raises its crest. Adult Little Blue Heron (22 in.) is more slender, uniformly dark all over, and with a pale base to its bill (see page 130).

CATTLE EGRET   This exotic bird (17 in.), a native of Africa, recently colonized North America. It is still spreading into new areas. It usually feeds with cattle, but it nests in colonies with other herons. Young birds are all white. Other white herons are the Snowy Egret (20 in.) with its slender black bill and legs and yellow feet, the immature Little Blue Heron (22 in.) with greenish legs and feet and a pale base to the bill, and the Great Egret (32 in.) with yellow bill, black legs and feet (page 130).

TUNDRA (WHISTLING) SWAN   This very large (36 in.) all-white bird migrates in V-formation from its arctic nesting ground to its winter quarters in coastal United States. In flight it is recognized by its muffled call. It feeds from the surface, using its long neck to reach

aquatic vegetation. The introduced Mute Swan (40 in.), found sparingly in the Great Lakes, in coastal waters, and some city parks, is told by its orange bill and gracefully curved neck.

CANADA GOOSE, a well-known and widely distributed bird, is recognized by its large size (16-25 in.), long black neck, and white cheeks. Geese swim with their necks straight up and fly in V-formation, with necks extended. They feed in ponds and estuaries, but also graze on grass and sprouting grain. The small, dark, arctic-nesting Brant (17 in.), which winters in flocks in coastal bays, has a small white neck stripe instead of white cheeks.

MALLARD This large (16 in.), common duck of ponds and sloughs has two white bars bordering its blue wing patch that identify both the colorful male and the mottled brown female. The green head and white neck ring are also good field marks of the male. Mallards, like

other surface-feeding ducks, take off in a vertical leap. They feed by tipping in shallow water. Mallards have been domesticated and often produce hybrids with other duck species.

AMERICAN BLACK DUCK This common marshland duck (16 in.) resembles the female Mallard, but is darker and has whiter wing linings. Males have bright red legs and yellowish bills; females are duller. Black Ducks prefer brackish water, especially in winter. The similar Mottled Duck (15 in.) is restricted to Florida and the Gulf Coast. The widespread Gadwall (14½ in.) is slightly smaller with a white belly and a small rectangular white patch on the black trailing edge of the wing.

WOOD DUCK (13½ in.) is told in flight by the white trailing edge of the wing, the long tail, short neck, and the bill held at a distinct downward angle. Note the large white eye ring of the female and young. Wood Ducks fly low, dodging around trees, where they

roost. The flying American Wigeon (14 in.) shows a large white patch on the forward edge of the wing, and the male has a white crown and a broad green band through the eye.

NORTHERN PINTAIL Spot the slim pintail (18½ in.) by the male's slender white neck and long, pointed tail. In all plumages flying birds show a white stripe on the trailing edge of the wing, which is the best field mark of the female. This common surface-feeding duck prefers fresh water. The tiny Green-winged Teal (10½ in.) has a broad green stripe across the face, contrasting with the plain brown head, and it has white borders before and behind the green wing patch.

CANVASBACK This diving duck (15 in.) swims low, often in large flocks. The long bill and sloping forehead are distinctive. In flight note the large size, and the wings set far back on the white body. It often flies in clusters of

V's. Female has olive head and neck. Smaller Redhead (14½ in.) has gray body, more rounded forehead. Closely related Lesser Scaup (12 in.) has violet head, white stripe down the extended wing.

COMMON MERGANSER Mergansers are loonlike diving ducks with narrow, cylindrical "toothed" bills. They fly low and prefer open water. White wing patches are visible in flight. The Common Merganser (18 in.) is strikingly white beneath. Note the sharply defined white throat of the female. The Red-breasted Merganser (16 in.) has a reddish breast and a larger crest and prefers salt water in winter. The smaller Hooded Merganser (13 in.) has a fan-shaped white crest.

AMERICAN COOT (12 in.) nests in marsh vegetation, but often winters in open water. It is the only ducklike bird with a chalky white bill. When disturbed it either dives or skits over the water with feet and wings.

The closely related Common Moorhen (or Florida Gallinule, 10½ in.) has a red bill and forehead and a white stripe under the wing. Both pump the neck when swimming.

KILLDEER (8 in.), a large upland plover, is told by its double breast band and (in flight) by its orange-brown rump and tail. It frequents open meadows and plowed fields, where its loud "killdeer" call resounds. It bobs its head as it walks. The young, which have only one breast band, leave the nest almost as soon as hatched. The much smaller Semi-palmated Plover (5¾ in.) is similar but lacks the bright rump. It too has only one breast band; it prefers mud flats and beaches.

COMMON SNIPE This shy bird (9 in.) of meadows and open fresh-water swamps rises high in the spring air at dusk and circles with an unforgettable "winnowing" sound; otherwise it stays close to vegetation. Field marks are very long bill, rather short legs, pointed wings, and zigzag flight. The plump American Woodcock (8¼ in.)

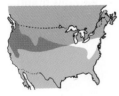

of moist woods and fields, a close relative, has rounded wings and a richer brown color. Dowitchers (10 in.), of mud flats and beaches, have a conspicuous white rump, and in spring are reddish-brown beneath.

LESSER YELLOWLEGS This gray-and-white sandpiper (8¾ in.) is one of our common shorebirds. In flight note its size, the white rump and tail, the slender, dark bill, and long, bright yellow legs. The Greater Yellowlegs (11 in.) is very similar but with a longer, slightly upturned bill. Willets (13½ in.) are still larger and plumper, with dark legs and with bold black-and-white wing markings in flight. Still larger are the Whimbrel (14 in.) with its long down-curved bill and the Marbled Godwit (16 in.) with its up-curved bill.

SPOTTED SANDPIPER (6¼ in.) This is our only sandpiper with a strongly spotted breast. In many inland localities this is the most common shorebird and the only breeding sandpiper. The spots are present only in the breeding season, but the teetering walk and the narrow

wing beats and low flight are distinctive. The Solitary Sandpiper (7 in.), seen during migration, has a white eye ring, and barred white feathers on the sides of the tail.

LEAST SANDPIPER Best known and smallest of the small sandpipers, this bird prefers mud flats and salt marshes. Note its small size (4¾ in.), rich brown back, breast band, yellowish legs, and slender, straight bill. The Semipalmated (5 in.) and Western (5¼ in.) Sandpipers, often found with the Least, have grayer backs, stouter bills, and black legs; the Western has a longer, heavier bill and tends to feed in deeper water. The larger White-rumped Sandpiper (6¼ in.) has a distinct white rump.

HERRING GULL (20 in.) is abundant along the Atlantic Coast and parts of the interior. It is a great scavenger. Black wing tips of adults contrast with gray wings and back. Legs are flesh-colored. Immature birds are dull gray-brown, becoming whiter with maturity. California and Ring-billed Gulls (17 in.) are smaller with dull yellowish or greenish legs; Ring-billed has a black ring on the bill. Laughing Gull (13 in.) on the East Coast and Franklin's Gull (11 in.) in the West have darker backs and black heads.

COMMON TERN Terns are smaller, slimmer, and more graceful than gulls; wings are slender and tails often deeply forked. They dive headlong into sea or lakes after fish. Common Tern (14 in.) is told by its black-tipped reddish bill, dusky wing tips, and deeply forked white tail. Forster's Tern (14 in.) is very similar but with orange bill, paler wing tips, and grayer tail. The tiny Least Tern (8½ in.) has a yellow bill and white forehead, the large Caspian Tern (20 in.) a heavy blood-red bill, and slightly forked tail.

TURKEY and BLACK VULTURES, valuable scavengers, soar high in the sky. Turkey Vultures (25 in.) soar with their long wings slightly above the horizontal; the naked red head completes identification of the adult. The smaller Black Vulture (at right, 22 in.) of the Southeast has round white patches on the underside of its wing tips, and it flaps more than does the Turkey Vulture. It has a dark head, as do young Turkey Vultures, and a very short square tail; it soars on horizontal wings.

OSPREY   The Osprey or Fish Hawk (22 in.) occurs around the world. It is smaller and slimmer than the eagles, and has a large black spot under the "elbow" of the wing. No other large hawk has as much white below. It flies with a characteristic backward bend at the "elbow." Its huge nest may be placed on an isolated tree, a tower, a channel marker, or a duck blind. The birds wheel and soar over lakes, bays, and oceans, plunging feet foremost after fish. Young are similar to adults.

BALD EAGLE Eagles are large, long-winged hawks that soar on horizontal wings. The white head and tail mark the adult Bald Eagle (32 in.). Younger birds are dark brown all over; it takes them several years to acquire adult plumage. Bald Eagles, our national emblem, are usually

found near water, as fish is their favorite food. The Golden Eagle (32 in.) of the West is all dark in all plumages except for the white base of its tail and a flash of white under each wing.

COOPER'S HAWK (15½ in.) is typically a woodland bird, rarely soaring in the open except when
migrating. Its short, rounded wings and long, rounded
tail identify it in flight. The little Sharp-shinned Hawk
(10½ in.) looks similar, but has a square-tipped tail and
smaller head. The large Northern
Goshawk (19 in.) has a light gray
breast, dark gray back, and white
line over the eye. Females of all are
much larger than males; breasts of
young are streaked lengthwise.

RED-TAILED HAWK   The Red-tail is a large (18 in.) soaring hawk. Its wings are broad and its tail is fan-shaped and chestnut-red above. Underparts are light except for a band of streaks across the belly. Young have a finely barred tail. Red-shouldered Hawk (16 in.), of wooded stream valleys, is rusty below with a distinctly banded tail. Other soaring hawks include the Broad-winged Hawk (13 in.) of northeastern woods with its prominently barred tail, and Swainson's Hawk (18 in.) of the West, with its broad, dark chest band.

AMERICAN KESTREL   This is the smallest (8½ in.) U.S. falcon—a hawk with long, pointed wings. It rarely soars. Note the rich reddish-brown back, tail, and crown. The female is told by narrow black bars on the tail. The slightly larger Merlin (12 in.) is uniformly dark above, heavily streaked below, and has broad black tail bars. The Peregrine Falcon (15 in.), which nests on cliffs and a few tall buildings, is a rare but wide-ranging species with heavy black mustache marks and a blue or brown back.

RING-NECKED PHEASANT This unmistakable Asiatic bird (27 in.) has been successfully introduced over much of the United States. It is a favorite game bird of farmlands, where it feeds on waste grain, occasionally causing local crop damage. The handsome male is unrivaled in its splendid coloring. The female is smaller, brown all over, but

with a short pointed tail that distinguishes it from the Ruffed Grouse and Prairie-Chickens (see next page). Pheasants and their relatives on the next two pages do not migrate.

RUFFED GROUSE This is an attractive chickenlike bird (14 in.) of the deep woods. It suddenly springs into the air with a loud whirring of wings. The drumming of the male is part of the spring courtship. The fan-shaped tail with its broad, dark terminal band is the best field mark. The Prairie-Chickens (14 in.) of the midwest prairies are finely barred all over with brown and white and have a black, rounded tail; they and the plain brown, narrow-tailed Sharp-tailed Grouse (15 in.) are restricted to open country.

NORTHERN BOBWHITE Everyone knows the bobwhite's call, but these small quail (8 in.) are hard to see in tall grass and weeds. Their small size, rich brown color, and stubby appearance make them easy to identify. Scaled, Gambel's, California, and Mountain Quails, all

8-9 in., have populations centered in New Mexico, Arizona, California, and Oregon, respectively; they are plain olive or gray on the back and have long head plumes. Females are duller than males.

ROCK DOVE (DOMESTIC PIGEON) is descended from the wild Rock Dove of European coastal cliffs. This chubby bird (11 in.) has a broad, fanned tail. Colors vary from slate-blue to brown to white. Their nesting habits make them unpopular tenants in cities. The large western Band-tailed Pigeon (13½ in.) has yellow legs and a pale tail band. The White-crowned Pigeon (11 in.) of the Florida keys is all dark with a white crown. The tiny Common Ground-Dove (5½ in.) of the far South has a short black tail and chestnut wings.

MOURNING DOVE Browner and slimmer than the Rock Dove and with a long, pointed tail, the Mourning Dove (10½ in.) nests in every state and province. It is named from its melancholy call: "Coo-ah, coo, coo, coo." The white tail border is conspicuous in flight. Flight is rapid, and this dove is prized as a favorite game

species in many states. The White-winged Dove (10 in.) of the Southwest is similar, but a large white wing patch is conspicuous in flight. The southwestern Inca Dove (6½ in.) is like a miniature Mourning Dove.

YELLOW-BILLED CUCKOO The slim, brown-and-white cuckoos are dovelike in appearance, but unlike doves they rarely perch in the open. They are among the few birds that eat hairy caterpillars. The Yellow-billed Cuckoo (11 in.) has a yellow lower bill, bright chestnut-brown wing patches, and large white tail spots. The more northern Black-billed Cuckoo (11 in.) has a black bill, plain brown wings, and indistinct tail spots. Young are similar to adults.

COMMON BARN-OWL This long-legged bird (14 in.) is unique among American owls, belonging to a separate family. The white, heart-shaped face and dark eyes identify it. The light buff plumage is conspicuous, but this owl is rarely seen by day, and the hissing call

that it gives at night is not often heard. It nests in barns, belfries, and hollow trees, and is important in controlling rodents injurious to orchards and garden crops. Its range is worldwide.

GREAT HORNED OWL (20 in.), aggressive and powerful, resembles a huge gray screech-owl. Its call is a series of five to seven deep hoots, all on the same pitch. The smaller, slender Long-eared Owl (13 in.) of the upper Midwest has similar ear tufts; it tends to give single hoots, wails, or screams. The eastern Barred Owl (17 in.) and western Spotted Owl (16 in.) have dark eyes, no ear tufts. The Barred Owl typically gives eight hoots, the Spotted Owl three or four.

EASTERN and WESTERN SCREECH-OWLS Re-
cently separated into two species, these closely related
nocturnal birds are told from other common owls by
their small size (8 in.) and presence of ear tufts. Plumage
of these two is almost identical, but gray and brown
color phases occur. Both species whistle rather than

screech. Keen eyesight and noise-
less flight enable them to prey on
field rodents. The terrestrial Bur-
rowing Owl (8 in.) of the prairies
and the Northern Saw-whet Owl (7
in.) of the North woods lack ear
tufts.

CHIMNEY SWIFT Swifts are almost always in the air, flying with a batlike flight. Distinctive, streamlined birds, they usually fly in groups and migrate in large flocks. The short spiny tails of Chimney Swifts (5 in.) prop them against inside walls of chimneys when resting.

There are three western swifts: Vaux's Swift (4½ in.), similar to the Chimney; White-throated Swift (6½ in.), of steep canyons; and the rare Black Swift (7 in.)—the last two colored as their names imply.

WHIP-POOR-WILL When resting on dead leaves the nocturnal Whip-poor-will (9 in.) is almost invisible— more often heard than seen. It rarely flies by day. A rounded tail, buffy-tipped in the female, and absence of white in the wing distinguish it from the nighthawks.

The southeastern Chuck-will's-widow (11 in.) has buff on the throat and under the tail. The small western Common Poor-will (7 in.) has only tiny square white patches at the corners of the tail.

COMMON NIGHTHAWK (9 in.), a close relative of the Whip-poor-will, has slender, pointed wings and a long tail with slightly notched tip. In flight note its distinguishing white wing patch. Nighthawks are constantly in the air at night, flying in a zigzag path, circling, diving, and banking as they catch flying insects. The lower-flying Lesser Nighthawk (8 in.) of the Southwest has the white band nearer the tip of a more rounded wing. Young are similar to adults.

RUBY-THROATED HUMMINGBIRD These eastern hummingbirds (3 in.) are gems of beauty and marvels in flight. They hover motionless, can fly backward, and may come to brightly colored tubes of sugar water. The female and young are white-throated. Western hummingbirds include the very similar Broad-tailed (3¾ in.)

of the southern Rockies; Anna's (3½ in.), with crown and throat metallic red; Black-chinned (3 in.) throughout the western mountains; and the brown-backed Rufous (3½ in.) of the Northwest.

BELTED KINGFISHER (12 in.) Where there are fish there are kingfishers, beating the air with irregular flaps, diving into water head first, and emerging with fish in their long beaks. Note the ragged crest and harsh rattling call. Illustration is of a female; the male lacks the chestnut on sides and breast. The tiny Green Kingfisher (7½ in.) of southern Texas has a dark green back and almost no crest.

RED-HEADED WOODPECKER Look for woodpeckers on tree trunks, using their strong bills to dig out wood-boring insects. The Red-headed (7½ in.) is the only eastern woodpecker with a totally red head. The solid black back and large white wing patches are good field marks. Young have brown heads. Male Red-bellied

Woodpecker (8½ in.) of the Southeast has entire crown and back of neck red, and black-and-white barring on the back. The western Acorn Woodpecker (8 in.) has black back, chin, and breast band.

NORTHERN FLICKER (10½ in.), large and brown, is identified by its bobbing flight, white rump, black breast band, and golden or salmon wing and tail linings. Like all woodpeckers it nests in a tree cavity, but this species often goes to the ground to eat ants. The eastern race (above) has yellow wing and tail shafts. The western Red-shafted and Gilded races have red mustache marks at the base of the bill. Young of all races are similar to adult males, but adult females lack the mustache.

YELLOW-BELLIED SAPSUCKER (7¾ in.) Sapsuckers feed on the soft inner bark and sap of trees. They dig rows of small holes that leave scars on trunks and branches. Note the vertical white patch on the black wing. The Red-breasted Sapsucker (7¼ in.) of the western mountain states is similar but with head and breast solid red. Williamson's Sapsucker (8¼ in.) of the Northwest is mostly black with a white rump, large white wing stripe, and yellow belly. Female sapsuckers lack red on throat.

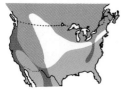

DOWNY WOODPECKER The Downy (5¾ in.) and Hairy (7½ in.) Woodpeckers are common and widespread and have similar plumage. The white stripe down the back is a good field mark for both. Only the males have the red spot on the back of the head. Young are like adults. The Hairy has a much heavier bill than the Downy Woodpecker, and its outer tail feathers are entirely white. The Downy feeds with chickadees, titmice, and nuthatches, and often visits feeding stations in winter for suet and seeds.

EASTERN KINGBIRD (6 ¾ in.) darts from its perch on a branch or fence in true flycatcher fashion. The white tip on the tail marks the Eastern species. The Gray Kingbird (7½ in.) of the Southeast has an oversized bill and a totally gray notched tail. The Western Kingbird (7 in.) is gray with a yellow belly and white outer tail feathers. The similar Cassin's Kingbird (7 in.) of the western mountains has only a narrow grayish tip to its tail. Young are similar to adults.

GREAT CRESTED FLYCATCHER is the only large (7 in.) eastern flycatcher with a rusty tail. The yellow belly and wing bars are good field marks. It is an orchard and forest bird. It typically uses shed snake skins in its nest, which is placed in a tree cavity or nest box. This flycatcher is told from the Western Kingbird by its tail color. The smaller, paler Ash-throated Flycatcher (6½ in.) replaces the Great Crested Flycatcher in the West. Young are like adults.

EASTERN PHOEBE (5¾ in.) If the persistent "fee-be" call doesn't identify this bird, its equally persistent tail-bobbing will. It is an active flycatcher, with no wing bars or eye ring. It nests in the shelter of a porch, out-building, or bridge. Say's Phoebe (6¼ in.) is a

western bird with rusty breast and belly. Eastern and Western Wood-Pewees (5¼ in.) look like small Eastern Phoebes but have two distinct wing bars and do not bob their tails.

LEAST FLYCATCHER is the smallest (4½ in.) eastern flycatcher. Its many close relatives share the eye ring and two whitish wing bars; they are best told apart by habitat and voice. Acadian Flycatcher nests in southeastern forests, Alder in northern alder swamps, Willow on brushy hillsides, Yellow-bellied in northeastern conifers. In the West the yellow-bellied Western Flycatcher is easily identified; but the drab Hammond's, Gray, and Dusky are best lumped under the group's generic name, *Empidonax*. Young are similar to adults.

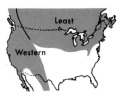

HORNED LARK Flocks of Horned Larks (6½ in.) feed in bare fields and along shores, walking as they feed. Note the black breast band, yellow throat, black tail, and, at close range, the "horns." Young birds are streaked. This and the Eurasian Skylark are true larks. Meadowlarks belong to the blackbird subfamily. The

Water Pipit (5½ in.), unrelated to the Horned Lark, is sometimes taken for it. The Water Pipit also walks, but has a lightly spotted buffy breast and a long bobbing tail with white outer feathers.

PURPLE MARTIN Martins are the largest (7 in.) and most conspicuous of the swallows, streamlined birds that do all of their feeding on the wing. In flight their wings are more triangular than other swallows'. Martins nest in colonies, most often in multi-celled martin boxes. The uniform dark color of the male identifies it. Females and young have grayish breast and white belly. The Northern Rough-winged Swallow (4¾ in.), which nests singly in drain pipes or holes in gravel banks, has a plain brown back and chest, no violet.

TREE SWALLOW Unbroken blue-black above and white below makes the Tree Swallow (5 in.) easy to pick out from a mixed flock of migrating swallows. Female is duller. Young birds are brown-backed. In cold weather this swallow can substitute bayberries for insects, so it

can winter farther north than other swallows. The western Violet-green Swallow (4¾ in.) is similar with a large white patch on each side of its rump. Swallows are usually found near water.

BARN SWALLOW (6 in.) This is the one swallow with a deeply forked "swallow tail." Note the chestnut forehead and throat, and the buff underparts. Female and young are duller with shorter tails. Nests in barns and under bridges. The Cliff Swallow (5 in.) is similar, but with short, square tail, buff rump, and white forehead. The Bank Swallow (4¾ in.), which nests in stream banks and gravel pits, is brown-backed with a brown band across its white breast.

BLACK-BILLED MAGPIE No other birds resemble the large black-and-white magpies with their sweeping tails. The two species, Black-billed (18 in.) and Yellow-billed (16 in.) Magpies, are distinguished by bill color and geography. The Yellow-billed Magpie lives only in the central California valleys. Magpies fly and feed in

flocks. Their mixed diet includes fruits, melons, and other crop plants. They often live around ranches, and occasionally these relatives of the crows become serious local pests.

AMERICAN CROW People often confuse two related birds with the familiar all-black American Crow (17 in.). The coastal Fish Crow (15 in.) is similar except for its short nasal call: "car, car." The large Common Raven (21 in.), rare in much of the East, has rough throat feathers and a croaking call. It soars in flight, showing the wedge-shaped tail tip.

BLUE JAY No other eastern bird is like the noisy blue, black, and white Blue Jay (10 in.). Of the western jays, Steller's (11 in.) has a black head, throat, and breast, and long black crest (page 18). The short-tailed, crestless Pinyon Jay (9 in.) is dull blue with a darker crown. The

Scrub Jay (10 in.), found commonly west of the Rockies and in central Florida, has a blue cap, wings, and tail, and a dull blue necklace across the whitish underparts. Young of all jays are similar to their parents.

WHITE-BREASTED NUTHATCH Nuthatches creep down tree trunks head first, and often visit feeding stations. The White-breasted Nuthatch (5 in.), with its white breast, throat, and face is common in deciduous woods. Other nuthatches prefer conifers. The northern Red-breasted Nuthatch (4 in.) has orange-brown under- parts and a dark line through the eye. The Brown-headed Nuthatch (4 in.) of southeast pine woods has a chocolate cap. The gray cap of the tiny western Pygmy Nuthatch (3½ in.) comes down to its eye.

BLACK-CAPPED CHICKADEE (4½ in.) The call of this plump bird is its name. Chickadees, constant visitors to feeding stations, often feed upside down. The smaller (4¼ in.) Carolina Chickadee of the Southeast has less buff on the sides, less white in the wing, and four or five notes in its whistled song instead of two or three. The

brown-capped Boreal Chickadee (4¼ in.) is a winter visitor along the Canadian border. The western Chestnut-capped Chickadee (4¼ in.) has a dull brown cap and a bright chestnut back.

TUFTED TITMOUSE   The pointed crest and the persistent whistled "peter, peter" call distinguish the Tufted Titmouse (5½ in.). It is told from chickadees by lack of the black bib, and from nuthatches by the stubby bill and perching habit. The cap and crest of Texas birds are black. The Plain Titmouse (5 in.) of the West lacks the rusty flanks. The slender, long-tailed Bushtit (3½ in.) of the arid West is plain gray-brown above, with no crest; crown is brown or gray. Young are similar to adults.

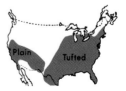

BROWN CREEPER This is the only small (4¾ in.) brown tree-creeping bird. Its underparts are white, its tail stiff. It works up the tree in a spiral, searching for insects and insect eggs that it digs out with its curved bill. Then it flies to the base of a nearby tree and climbs up again. As their calls are high-pitched and their colors blend well with bark, these birds may be hard to detect.

 They prefer open mature woods, nesting under loose bark. They feed in small flocks of chickadees, kinglets, and woodpeckers. In winter they like suet feeders placed on tree trunks. Young are like adults.

HOUSE WREN Wrens are small, brown birds that usually carry their tails upright. The well-known House Wren (4¼ in.) is a garden bird that lacks distinct head markings. The tiny northern Winter Wren (3¼ in.) has a dark belly and shorter tail. Carolina Wren (4¾ in.) of the Southeast has a large white eye stripe and a ruddy back. Western wrens include Bewick's Wren (4½ in.) with a white eye stripe and a long tail with narrow white border, Canyon Wren (4½ in.) with white breast and contrasting dark belly, Rock Wren (4¾ in.) with faint breast streaks and buff-fringed tail, and the huge Cactus Wren (6½ in.) of the deserts.

RUBY-CROWNED KINGLET   Kinglets are among our smallest birds (3¾ in.) and are doubly attractive because they are primarily winter visitors. Their small, chunky bodies, stubby tails, and dull, olive color are distinctive. The frequent flicking of wings is characteristic of kinglets. The red crown of the Ruby-crowned Kinglet is often hidden, but the large eye ring will distinguish

this species when its ruby crown does not show. Female lacks the ruby crown. Kinglets breed in northern spruce-fir forests. In winter they are often seen in shrubbery around buildings.

GOLDEN-CROWNED KINGLET (3½ in.) is the more showy of our two American species. The female has a golden crown bordered with black and white. The male has an additional orange stripe through the center of the golden crown. These kinglets are often seen feeding on the branches of firs, spruce, and other conifers, but in winter they also use deciduous woods. They eat insects, so are not attracted to feeding stations, although they are often found with chickadees, nuthatches, creepers, and woodpeckers in winter. Common call is three to five very high notes on the same pitch.

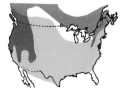

BLUE-GRAY GNATCATCHER (4 in.) With its long, white-bordered tail, gnatcatchers look like miniature mockingbirds. Common in the South, but seldom seen because of its preference for treetops in moist woods. The blue back and the white eye ring aid identification; so does its habit of jerking its tail. Female and young lack black stripe over eye. The Black-tailed Gnatcatcher (4 in.) of south-western deserts has a black cap (male); the tail of both sexes is black beneath instead of mostly white.

EASTERN BLUEBIRD (5½ in.) is an early spring migrant in the North. It is a thrush, as the spotted breast of the young testifies. No other blue bird in the East has chestnut-brown breast. The Western Bluebird (5½ in.) has chestnut on the back as well. The adult male Mountain Bluebird (6 in.) of the Rockies has a lighter sky-blue back, pale blue breast, and white belly. Bluebirds may be attracted to nesting boxes with 1½ in. holes. Female and young bluebirds are much duller.

WOOD THRUSH The spotted thrushes are typically woodland birds. Wood Thrushes (7 in.) are common in deciduous woods. They are recognized by their chestnut-brown backs, brighter heads, heavily spotted breasts, and clear, flutelike songs. The Veery (6 in.), which requires moist woods, also has a bright unmarked

red-brown back, but with head and tail the same color as the back; it has only faint spotting on its breast. The long-tailed Brown Thrasher (page 91) has a streaked breast, but its eye is yellow.

HERMIT THRUSH Famous songster of the mountains and the North woods, the Hermit Thrush (7 in.) reverses the Wood Thrush pattern. Its tail, which it slowly raises and lowers, is much brighter than its back. The breast is less spotted than the Wood Thrush's, but more so than the Veery's. Other thrushes have dull, olive-brown backs and tails. Swainson's Thrush (6¼ in.) has a buff eye ring and buff cheeks. The northern Gray-cheeked Thrush (6¼ in.), an eastern migrant, has gray cheeks and no eye ring. Young of all are like adults.

AMERICAN ROBIN   One of the most common native birds of towns and villages, the robin (8½ in.) nests in every state except Hawaii and in every Canadian province. It is the largest of the thrushes, and young robins have the heavily spotted breasts that are characteristic of thrushes. Females are similar but duller. Colonists named the robin after a small European thrush with a much redder breast. The Varied Thrush (8 in.) of the Pacific states is similar to our robin but has a black breast band (page 130).

GRAY CATBIRD   Not quite as handsome as the mockingbird, the Gray Catbird (7¾ in.) sings almost as well, but is a poor imitator. Its name comes from its mewing call. It feeds and nests low in shrubs and vines, often near houses or in moist thickets. Catbirds are slaty-gray except for the black cap and a chestnut patch under the base of the tail. The slender bill and long, rounded tail will separate the catbird from other dark birds its size. Young are like adults.

NORTHERN MOCKINGBIRD "Listen to the mockingbird..." goes the song, and the mockingbird (9 in.) is, indeed, worth hearing. Its song imitates other birds' songs perfectly, with original phrases added. Mockingbirds nest around homes, perch on chimneys and television antennas. White patches on wings and tail are conspicuous in flight. The Loggerhead Shrike (7 in., page 93), which also perches on wires and fences, is chunkier, with a thick bill and black mask.

BROWN THRASHER   Related to the mockingbirds, thrashers have the same long rounded tails; most have down-curved bills. They feed and nest near the ground. The widespread Brown Thrasher (10 in.) is the richest chestnut above and streaked with brown below. The only western thrasher with heavy streaks, Sage Thrasher (7 in.), has white tips on its outer tail feathers. Le Conte's Thrasher (9¼ in.) is an ashy-gray desert bird with a plain breast. The California Thrasher (10 in.) is dark brown and unstreaked with a long down-curved bill; no wing bars.

CEDAR WAXWING (5¾ in.) These warm-brown, crested birds cannot be mistaken, especially when a whole flock is feeding on cherries or mulberries. Watch for the wide yellow tail band. Young are faintly streaked below and have less crest. The grayer Bohemian Waxwing (6¼ in.) of the Northwest has bright cinnamon

instead of white under the base of its tail. Bohemian Waxwings nest in western Canada, but occasionally winter in the north central states. Their irregular appearance makes them mystery birds.

LOGGERHEAD SHRIKE (7 in.) Shrikes feed on insects, rodents, and small birds. They often hang their prey on thorns or barbed-wire fences. Resembling mockingbirds, the shrikes are chunkier, have a black eye mask, and a heavy hooked bill. Their rapid wing beats and bounding flight are distinctive. The Northern Shrike is a larger species (8 in.) with a faintly barred breast that is seen only in winter in the northern states. Its black mask is divided by the bill, which is light below. Young are browner than adults.

EUROPEAN STARLING (6 in.) Introduced into New York in 1890, starlings have been spreading ever since. In some places they are a nuisance and even a pest. But they are handsome birds, given to musical song and mimicry. Sunlight on their plumage makes a rainbow of

colors. Note the short tail, plump body, and (in spring and summer) the yellow bill. Young birds are uniform brown with dark bills, and adults in winter are speckled with white.

Yellow Warbler

WARBLERS

The wood-warblers are a strictly American subfamily of the large bird family known as the Emberizids, which also includes the tanagers, grosbeaks, sparrows, black-birds, and orioles. Fifty-eight of the 109 species of wood-warblers occur in the United States and include some of our most beautiful birds. To many, warblers are the most exciting birds to watch because of their many species, bright colors, distinctive songs, and migratory habits. Most winter in the tropics and migrate north to their breeding grounds in April and May; as many as 25 species may be found on a warm May morning. Learning the songs from records or tapes will help beginners find additional species.

Warblers are small, active woodland birds with slender, straight bills for catching crawling or flying insects. Males migrate a few days ahead of the duller-colored females. The best time to see them is before the trees are in full leaf. Young birds and autumn adults of many species are more drab and less easy to identify. By November most warblers have left for their winter homes in the tropics, but the Yellow-rumped Warbler (page 100) can be found all winter in southern and coastal states.

YELLOW WARBLER   This is the only warbler with yellow spots on the tail. The male has distinctive chestnut streaks on his breast. The Yellow Warbler (4 in.) prefers

shrubs or low trees, so is easily seen. The Orange-crowned Warbler (4¼ in.) of the West is dull yellow-green all over, with a small orange crown patch and no wing bars or tail spots.

BLACK-AND-WHITE WARBLER   Only two eastern warblers are striped black and white: the common Black-and-white Warbler (4½ in.) and the Blackpoll (4½ in.), which has a solid black crown and is seen only during

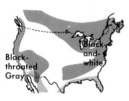

migration. The Black-and-white feeds along tree trunks and large branches. Female and young lack the black throat. The western Black-throated Gray Warbler has a plain, almost unstreaked back.

BLACK-THROATED BLUE WARBLER   This warbler (4½ in.) is really well named. No other North American bird has a blue back and black throat. The only distinguishing mark of the plain olive female is the small white

wing spot. The Black-throated Green Warbler (4¼ in.) of the East has a yellow-green back and golden face. The Cerulean Warbler (4 in.) of the Midwest is blue above, white below with a narrow black necklace.

COMMON YELLOWTHROAT (4¼ in.) This is a warbler of marshes and moist wayside shrubbery. The black mask and yellow throat mark the male. The female has the yellow throat but no mask. Its whitish belly and

absence of wing bars aid identification. The Kentucky Warbler (4½ in.) of southeastern woodlands has a large yellow eye ring, black crown and sideburns, and entirely yellow underparts.

OVENBIRD This is another ground-loving warbler often seen walking in the leaves, its tail bobbing. The Ovenbird (5 in.) resembles a small thrush: plain olive-brown above with a streaked breast. The orange crown

with black borders and a narrow eye ring make identification positive. Its "teacher, teacher, teacher" song is easy to remember. Watch for it in eastern deciduous forests. Young lack the orange crown.

NORTHERN WATERTHRUSH These plump warblers stay near the ground in swamps and brooks. The Northern Waterthrush (5 in.) has a distinct yellowish cast to the heavily streaked underparts, and usually a buffy eye

line. The more southern Louisiana Waterthrush (5¼ in.) is whiter below, except for the buffy lower flanks; its throat is unstreaked, the eye line white and broader. Both species teeter like sandpipers.

YELLOW-RUMPED WARBLER The yellow rump, crown, and side patches mark this warbler (4¾ in.). Female, young, and winter birds are browner. Western birds have yellow throats. This species migrates earlier in the spring and later in the fall than other common warblers. It is often found in large

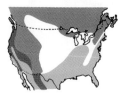

flocks. The yellow-rumped Magnolia Warbler (4¼ in.) of the East has a black-streaked yellow breast, much more white in wings and tail. Female, young are browner.

AMERICAN REDSTART The orange and black male (4½ in.) is a striking bird of moist deciduous forests. The female is yellow and olive-gray, but with the same

pattern. Redstarts continually flit about and catch insects flycatcher fashion. The Painted Redstart (4½ in.) of evergreen forests in Arizona and New Mexico has a red breast, flashy white wing and tail patches.

WILSON'S WARBLER A small (4¼ in.), very active warbler, unbroken yellow below, plain olive-yellow above. There are no wing bars or tail spots. The female lacks the black cap. It prefers moist thickets and swamps

and is especially fond of willows. Hooded Warbler (4½ in.) of southeastern forests is similar except male has a black head and throat with yellow face; both sexes have white tail spots.

RED-EYED VIREO Vireos are larger and less active than warblers. The Red-eyed (5 in.), common in deciduous forests, has a gray crown bordered with black, a broad white line above the red eye, and no wing bars. The dark-eyed Warbling Vireo (4¾ in.) lacks dark head marks. A pale yellow eye ring and two wing bars help

identify the White-eyed Vireo (4½ in.). The Yellow-throated Vireo (5 in.) of the East and the bluish-headed Solitary Vireo (4¾ in.) have broad wing bars and eye rings. All young have brown eyes.

SCARLET TANAGER (6¼ in.) The male is our only red bird with black wings. The female is uniform yellow-green with dusky wings. The male Summer Tanager (6½ in.) of the South is entirely red, its mate orange-yellow. It prefers pine woods, while the Scarlet uses mixed or deciduous. The Western Tanager (6¼ in.) is bright yellow, with red only on the head; this is our only tanager with wing bars. Tanagers are told from orioles by their shorter, heavier bills.

NORTHERN CARDINAL   The cardinal (7¾ in.) is
the only eastern red bird with a crest. The heavy red
bill, with black at the base, is a good field mark. The
light brown female has the crest and red bill, but little
red on the body. Young have dusky bills. Cardinals are
common in shrubbery, hedgerows, and wood margins.

In recent years the cardinal has
gradually spread northward. The
crested Pyrrhuloxia (7½ in.) of the
Southwest is mostly gray with red
face, crest, breast, and tail, and
the general cardinal shape.

ROSE-BREASTED GROSBEAK The male (7¼ in.), nearly all black and white, flashes a deep rose patch on its breast. The female is streaked yellow-brown and white like an overgrown sparrow. Like all grosbeaks they have heavy conical bills. The closely related Black-headed Grosbeak (7¼ in.) of the west also has the black head and back, but its entire underparts are orange-brown. The Evening Grosbeak (7¼ in.) of the North and the western mountains is a brilliant yellow with black-and-white wings and tail.

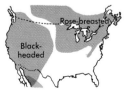

INDIGO BUNTING   This is our only small bird (4½ in.) that is entirely blue. Female and young are uniform gray-brown. They live in hedgerows and wood margins. The southern Blue Grosbeak (6¼ in.) is much larger with chestnut wing bars and a much heavier bill. Other buntings are also splashes of brilliant color. The Lazuli Bunting (5½ in.) of the West is similar to the Indigo, but has

white wing bars, chestnut breast, and white belly. The male Painted Bunting (4½ in.) of the South is a showy combination of red below and blue and green above; but the female is plain yellow-green.

RUFOUS-SIDED TOWHEE This towhee (7¼ in.) may be told by its "chewink" call and by its plumage. The black back and tail (white tip), white belly, and chestnut side patches are good field marks. Eyes of the adult are bright red (white in southeastern birds). The female is brown instead of black. This species nests in thickets within both coniferous and decid-uous woods. A western form has many small white spots on the wings and back. All towhees are ground-feeders that scratch vigorously in dead leaves for insects and seeds.

BROWN TOWHEE This western towhee (7¼ in.) is plain brown above, gray below, with a chestnut cap and with orange-brown on the throat and under the tail. Favored habitats are suburban shrubbery, chaparral, and stream borders. The shy Abert's Towhee (7¾

in.) of Southwest deserts is chestnut-brown all over, with a black face. The Green-tailed Towhee (6¼ in.) of western mountains has a green back, reddish crown, white throat, and gray sides.

Chipping Sparrow

SPARROWS

Worldwide there are nearly 300 species of sparrows, of which 52 have been recorded in North America north of Mexico. Towhees, juncos, and some less well-known birds such as grassquits and longspurs are included in these totals. The only ones discussed here are birds that occur over much of the continent and are likely to be found by beginners.

Sparrows are small to medium-sized birds with stout conical bills adapted for crushing seeds, which are their main diet. Seed-eaters have a better chance for winter survival in the North than do insect-eaters, so sparrows are conspicuous winter residents in areas where daytime winter temperatures are likely to remain below freezing for several consecutive days.

Most sparrows have streaked backs. Head and breast patterns can be used to identify most species. Each species has its own particular nesting habitat in summer, but during migration and in winter several species often flock together. Sparrows are short-distance migrants, wintering largely within the United States and southern Canada. They arrive on their breeding grounds early in spring. Most species prefer fields rather than woodlands.

FIELD SPARROW This common sparrow (5 in.) of brushy fields displays a reddish-brown crown; its plain breast, pink bill and legs, and broad gray eye ring clinch its identification. Its song is an accelerating series of slurred whistles. Compare the Field Sparrow with the American Tree, Chipping, and Swamp Sparrows, which have the same reddish cap.

AMERICAN TREE SPARROW The bright reddish cap together with the single dark breast spot identifies the American Tree Sparrow (5¼ in.). Note also that the bill is dark above, yellowish below. The sweet song is rarely heard in its winter range. This bird is not related to the Eurasian Tree Sparrow (5 in.), which has been introduced into southern Illinois and which looks like a House Sparrow with a small black cheek patch and brown crown.

VESPER SPARROW White outer tail feathers distinguish the Vesper Sparrow (5½ in.), a bird of large open fields. Otherwise, except for the small chestnut wing patch, this bird resembles the Song Sparrow (page 114). Other small birds with white outer tail feathers are the slender-billed long-tailed pipits and the Dark-eyed Junco. The Lark Sparrow (5¾ in.) of the West has a broad white fringe around the tail, a large chestnut ear patch, and a central breast spot.

CHIPPING SPARROW   This small sparrow (4½ in.) is told by its reddish crown, clear white underparts, white line over the eye, black line through the eye, and black bill. Young have streaked crowns with little or no red. The song is a rapid series of unmusical "chips" on

the same pitch. The Chipping Sparrow prefers lawns, golf courses, and other short-grass habitats.

WHITE-CROWNED SPARROW   The black-and-white crown, erect posture, plain gray breast and throat, and pink or yellowish bill identify this sparrow (5¾ in.). Young have brown and buff head stripes. Western birds use suburban habitats, but eastern birds prefer hedge-

rows bordered by large fields. The Golden-crowned Sparrow (6¼ in.), which winters in the Pacific states, differs by having a dull yellow crown bordered with black.

WHITE-THROATED SPARROW   This bird (5¾ in.) is told from the preceding by a distinct white throat and a small spot of yellow before the eye. It lacks the erect posture and gray hind neck of the White-crowned Sparrow. Its whistled "Old Sam Peabody Peabody Peabody"

song is familiar in the North woods in summer, and can also be heard on warm winter mornings. In winter it prefers wood margins and thickets, and is never found far from cover.

SONG SPARROW A large brown center spot on a boldly streaked breast, and a rather long, rounded tail that it pumps as it flies, are the field marks of the Song Sparrow (5½ in.). Its melodious, varied song, one of the first signs of spring, is easy to recognize. At all seasons Song Sparrows are found in hedgerows, shrub-

bery, and weedy fields. The smaller Lincoln's Sparrow (4¾ in.), most common in the West, is similar but with a buff breast band crossed by fine dark streaks.

SWAMP SPARROW (5 in.) Note the Swamp Sparrow's white throat, red-brown crown, plain gray breast, and rounded tail. The rusty wings, dark bill, and the

broad gray stripe over the eye (buffy in young birds) will confirm the identification. It prefers moist brushy habitats at all seasons. Its song is a slow musical trill.

FOX SPARROW Our largest true sparrow (6¼ in.), this bird is recognized by its bright red-brown tail and its heavily streaked breast. Though a little like the Hermit Thrush (page 87) in size and markings, the Fox

Sparrow has a heavier bill and larger, more conspicuous breast streaks. It frequents woods and thickets, and it scratches in dry leaves with both feet at once like a towhee.

DARK-EYED JUNCO This even gray bird (5¼ in.) with clear white outer tail feathers and a whitish bill is usually seen on or near the ground, feeding on seeds. The female is browner, especially on the back and sides. Juncos are common nesting birds in the North woods, preferring conifers. They are attracted to feeders in winter. Western races tend to have blacker heads and more rusty backs. A large race (6 in.) in the Black Hills of South Dakota has white wing bars. Adult Yellow-eyed Juncos of Arizona have yellow eyes.

EASTERN MEADOWLARK This bird (8½ in.) prefers pastures, meadows, and grain fields. The very similar Western Meadowlark (8½ in.) is slightly paler on the back, and the yellow of the throat goes higher on the cheek. The only other large songbirds with white outer tail feathers are the mockingbird and the shrikes. Note the black "V" on the yellow breast of the meadowlarks. Young of both species are like the adults. The Western Meadowlark's song is louder and more flutelike than the simple whistle of the Eastern bird.

Western Eastern

BOBOLINK The male (6 in.), the only North American songbird that is light above, all-black below, is easy to identify. However, the female and the male in fall are sparrowlike, with buff breasts and black-and-buff stripes on the crown. In summer it eats insects in hayfields, but

in fall it may damage rice crops. The other grains it eats are of no commercial value. The Bobolink winters in South America. Its song is one of the most beautiful of bird songs.

RED-WINGED BLACKBIRD The male (7¼ in.) is unique with its red shoulders, margined with buff. The female is dusky brown above with a heavily streaked breast and generally with no hint of the red shoulder. The Tricolored Blackbird (7½ in.) of California's central valleys has deeper red shoulders with a white margin. Both species are abundant marsh and field birds, nesting in reeds, cattails, and shrubs. They form large flocks during fall, winter, and spring.

BREWER'S BLACKBIRD (8 in.) This is the blackbird of western ranches and corrals. The yellow eye of the male and the purplish tinge to its head feathers are field marks. It walks with its wings slightly drooping. The female is plain brownish gray with brown eyes. The Rusty

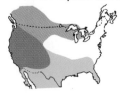

Blackbird (8 in.) of the East is similar, but with white eyes and rusty tips to its feathers. The Rusty Blackbird seldom flocks with other blackbirds; it is usually found in swamp forests instead of in fields.

COMMON GRACKLE Grackles are abundant, large blackbirds with long wedge-shaped tails. The Common Grackle (10-12 in.) is a familiar suburban and farmland bird that nests in colonies in evergreen trees. Note the iridescent plumage of the male. The Boat-tailed Grackle (12-16 in.) is found along the coast from Delaware to Texas, and the Great-tailed Grackle (12-16 in.) is becoming abundant in the southern Great Plains. Female grackles are much smaller than males.

BROWN-HEADED COWBIRD (6½ in.) has the unfortunate habit of always laying its eggs in nests of other birds. Its eggs hatch sooner than those of its host; only the fast-growing cowbirds survive. The cowbird is our smallest blackbird, and the only one with a brown head.

It gets its name from its habit of feeding with cattle. Like other blackbirds, they walk, but they hold their tails higher when walking than do their relatives. The female is uniform mouse-gray.

NORTHERN ORIOLE   The brilliant male (7 in.) is a showy bird. The female is olive above, dull orange-yellow below, with two pale wing bars; she selects a tall shade tree for her hanging nest. Western males have orange on the sides of the head and over the eye. The Orchard Oriole (6 in.), east of the Rockies, is similar, but is brick red, not orange; the female Orchard Oriole is greenish-yellow. Young orioles are similar to females. Other orioles are in the Southwest.

PURPLE FINCH The male Purple Finch (5½ in.) is old-rose in color, not purple. Females are sparrowlike, streaked brown and white with a distinctive dark streak at the side of the throat. Both sexes have the heavy seed-crushing bill, pale line over the eye, and notched tail. Feeders with sunflower seeds attract flocks of Purple Finches in winter. In the West, the similar Cassin's Finch

(6 in.) is recognized by the contrast between its brilliant red crown and the browner hind neck and back. Both species nest in conifers but are often found in deciduous trees and shrubs in winter.

HOUSE FINCH This abundant suburban bird (5¼ in.) is easily attracted to feeding stations. A native of the West, a flock was released on Long Island in the 1950's, and the descendents are now spreading rapidly in the East. The male has more brown on the wings, back, and breast than the Purple Finch. The female is nondescript, more faintly streaked than the female Purple Finch, and without the prominent line over the eye and the dark streak beside the throat. The bill is nearly as large as the Purple Finch's, the tail less notched.

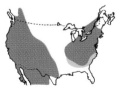

AMERICAN GOLDFINCH The yellow body, black cap and wings mark the American Goldfinch (4¼ in.). In flight it is recognized by its roller-coaster flight and its clear song. It is a bird of weedy fields and meadows, feeding near the ground, and nesting in young trees. Female, young, and winter males are dull yellow-brown, with wing bars but no black on the head. The western

Lesser Goldfinch (3¾ in.) is similar, with black crown, but dark (green or black) back and duller yellow breast. Sunflower or thistle seeds will attract goldfinches to feeding stations.

HOUSE SPARROW This bird (5¼ in.), misnamed English Sparrow, is a native of Europe belonging to the Old World Sparrow family. Imported from England in 1850, it became established, spread rapidly, and is now widespread. The gray crown and black throat of the male are characteristic, as are the unstreaked brown crown and broad buff line over the eye of the female. Unlike our native sparrows, the House Sparrow nests in cavities and bird boxes. It is an aggressive species, driving native birds from feeders and nest boxes.

MIGRATIONS OF BIRDS

Arctic Tern (13 in.): grayish; red bill; black cap.

Most swimming birds that depend on flying or crawling insects cannot winter in cold climates. Some seed-eaters also migrate. Some birds migrate by day, others by night. No one knows just how birds find their way from their summer to their winter homes.

Migrations north and south are best known. Some birds move only a few hundred miles from their breeding to their winter range; others cover several thousand. Scarlet Tanagers travel from Peru to northern U.S.

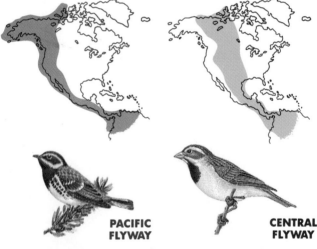

PACIFIC FLYWAY

CENTRAL FLYWAY

Townsend's Warbler (4¼ in.) flies from Alaska and Yukon to Central America.

Dickcissel (5¾ in.) migrates in enormous numbers from our grasslands to South America.

and back. Some warblers, vireos, and flycatchers travel even farther. The champion migrant is the Arctic Tern; some breed in the Arctic and winter in the Antarctic, 11,000 miles away. They fly over 25,000 miles a year and cross the Atlantic in their migration.

Four North American flyways form connecting paths between northern breeding grounds and wintering areas in the southern United States, Mexico, Cuba, and South America. Their use by waterfowl is best known, though most migrating birds use them. Flyways overlap in the breeding grounds, though each tends to have its own population.

The periods of spring and fall migrations are the times you will see the most birds. See pages 131-153 for when to look for migrants.

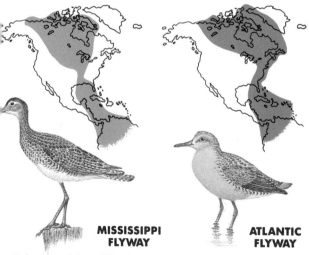

MISSISSIPPI FLYWAY

ATLANTIC FLYWAY

Upland Sandpiper (10 in.) migrates from the Arctic and the prairies to central South America.

Red Knot (8½ in.) concentrates on the Atlantic coast enroute from the Arctic to Chile.

Varied Thrush (8 in.): Robin-like, black bar on orange breast.

Evening Grosbeak (7¼ in.): larger than goldfinch; huge beak.

Besides north and south migrations, vertical movements occur in high mountains. Summer residents nest high among spruce and fir in summer, later moving down to foothills and valleys for more dependable winter food.

Many species normally migrating farther north breed at high elevations in the mountains. Another pattern is

that shown by young herons and eagles. Soon after they leave the nest, they wander northward. By late summer or early fall many are hundreds of miles north of their nesting grounds. Before winter they go south again.

Left: **Great Egret** (32 in.), a large heron, all white; black legs, yellow bill. Right: **Little Blue Heron** (22 in.), smaller than Great Blue (p. 23). Legs greenish. Young white; blue tint on wings.

The tables on pages 132-153 give concisely, for each bird illustrated, a wealth of facts on migration, nests and eggs, and feeding habits.

The information on migration is given by key cities: DC—Washington, D.C.; NY—New York; B—Boston; StL—St. Louis; SF—San Francisco; P—Portland, Oreg. You can estimate the arrival of birds in your region from dates for the nearest key city. There is about a week's difference between DC and NY and between NY and B for most migrating birds.

Birds found in an area the year round are listed as "permanent residents." For "summer residents" (SR), which come north in the spring, stay all summer, and depart in the fall, the table gives the average dates of arrival and departure. Average dates for "winter residents" (WR) are similarly given. Finally, some birds come north in the spring and, after staying a while, continue northward. These can be seen for only a few weeks in spring and fall. These birds are "transients" (Tr). Approximate dates for all birds are given in abbreviated form: E, M, and L stand for "early," "middle," and "late." "E-Apr" means early April and "M-Oct" stands for middle October.

Local weather, food supply, and other factors influence arrival and departure of birds. After several years, your own personal records may prove a better local guide than the abbreviated data given here, especially if you compare dates with those recorded by other observers in your county.

Birds and their nests and eggs are protected by federal and state laws. We do not encourage visiting nests, but if a nest is found, the information on pages 132-153 will help to identify the owner.

Page	Name	Migration		Eggs	
		Arrive	Depart	Size (in.)	N
21	Common Loon	DC E-Oct B L-Sept StL E-Apr SF E-Oct	WR M-May WR L-May Tr L-Nov WR E-May	3.5 × 2.2 Variable; greenish or d⟨⟩ brown with faint bla⟨⟩ spots.	
22	Pied-billed Grebe	DC M-Mar B E-Apr StL M-Mar P Permanent Resident	SR L-Oct SR M-Oct SR L-Nov	1.7 × 1.1 Very light blue-gre⟨⟩ darker or buff; u⟨⟩ marked.	4
23	Great Blue Heron	NY E-Apr B E-Apr StL E-Mar SF Permanent Resident	SR L-Nov SR M-Nov SR L-Nov	2.4 × 1.8 Pale bluish green to d⟨⟩ blue; unmarked.	3
24	Green-backed Heron	DC M-Apr B L-Apr StL M-Apr SF M-Mar	SR E-Oct SR M-Sept SR L-Sept SR L-Oct	1.5 × 1.1 Pale greenish or greeni⟨⟩ blue; unmarked.	3
25	Cattle Egret	DC M-Apr NY L-Apr StL E-May	Tr M-Oct SR E-Oct SR L-Aug	1.8 × 1.3 Very pale green.	3
26	Tundra Swan	DC M-Nov StL M-Oct SF E-Oct	WR M-Apr WR L-Apr WR E-Apr	4.3 × 2.8 White or pale yellow.	2
27	Canada Goose	DC L-Sept B L-Sept StL E-Oct P M-Sept	WR M-Apr Tr L-Apr WR M-Apr WR M-May	3.4 × 2.3 Cream to dull greeni⟨⟩ white. Later buffy a⟨⟩ mottled.	4-⟨⟩
28	Mallard	DC Permanent Resident NY E-Oct StL E-Sept P Permanent Resident	WR M-Apr WR E-May	2.3 × 1.6 Pale greenish to grayi⟨⟩ buff.	6-⟨⟩
29	American Black Duck	DC Permanent Resident NY Permanent Resident B Permanent Resident StL L-Oct	WR E-Apr	2.3 × 1.7 Grayish white to gree⟨⟩ ish buff. Similar to M⟨⟩ lard.	6-⟨⟩
30	Wood Duck	DC L-Feb NY M-Mar StL M-Feb P Permanent Resident	SR M-Nov SR E-Nov SR L-Nov	2.0 × 1.6 Dull cream to buff.	8-⟨⟩

Nests		Food
Materials	Location	
Vegetable debris.	On ground on small island or near shore of lake or pond.	Mainly fish; crabs, some insects and marine algae.
Decaying vegetation.	In shallow water. Floating among rushes in lakes and ponds.	Crayfish, crustaceans, small fish, and insects.
Sticks.	High up in tree or cliff near water.	Mainly fish; also crustaceans, frogs, and mice.
Sticks and twigs.	In trees, but near water; occasionally on ground.	Mainly fish, aquatic insects and crustaceans.
Sticks and twigs.	In trees or shrubs, 5-12 ft. up.	Insects, especially grasshoppers; frogs, spiders. Also ticks.
Grasses, sedges, and mosses.	6 ft. diameter mound in marshes or wet grassy meadows.	Stems, seeds, and roots of aquatic plants.
Twigs, weeds, grasses, lined with down.	On dry ground near water, often on small island.	Pondweeds, grasses; seeds of wheat, barley, sedges.
Reeds and grasses, lined with down.	On ground among high grass or reeds; usually near water.	Pondweeds, wild rice and other seeds; aquatic insects.
Grasses, weeds, leaves; feather lining.	Usually on ground in grass or brush. Sometimes far from water.	Same as Mallard.
Grasses, twigs, leaves; down-lined.	Up to 60 ft. above ground; in a hole in tree or stump.	Wild rice, pondweeds, acorns, seeds, and fruits; some insects.

Page	Name	Migration		Eggs	
		Arrive	Depart	Size (in.)	No.
31	Northern Pintail	NY M-Sept StL L-Sept SF E-Sept P Permanent Resident	WR M-Apr Tr L-Apr WR L-Apr	2.2 × 1.5 Similar to Mallard.	5-12
32	Canvasback	DC E-Nov NY M-Oct StL L-Oct SF M-Oct	WR E-Apr WR M-Apr WR L-Apr WR L-Apr	2.5 × 1.6 Olive gray or dull green.	6-10
33	Common Merganser	DC M-Nov B M-Oct StL M-Nov P Permanent Resident	WR E-Apr WR L-Apr WR M-Apr	2.5 × 1.7 Pale buff; unmarked.	6-17
34	American Coot	DC M-Oct NY E-Oct StL M-Feb SF Permanent Resident	WR E-May Tr L-Nov SR M-Nov	1.9 × 1.3 Light buff, speckled with dark brown or black.	8-12
35	Killdeer	NY E-Mar B L-Mar StL L-Feb SF Permanent Resident	SR E-Nov SR L-Oct SR L-Nov	1.5 × 1.1 Buff or darker; heavily spotted or mottled.	4
36	Common Snipe	DC M-Sept StL L-Feb SF E-Sept P Permanent Resident	Tr E-May Tr L-Nov WR E-May	1.6 × 1.2 Pale olive to brown darker spots and specks.	4
37	Lesser Yellowlegs	DC E-Apr NY E-Apr StL E-Apr SF E-Aug	Tr M-Oct Tr E-Oct Tr E-Oct Tr E-May	1.6 × 1.1 Buffy with bold blotches of chocolate and blackish.	3-5
38	Spotted Sandpiper	DC M-Apr B E-May StL M-Apr P L-Apr	SR L-Sept SR M-Sept SR E-Oct SR M-Oct	1.3 × 0.9 White to cream; heavily marked with dark brown and black.	4
39	Least Sandpiper	DC L-Apr StL E-Apr SF E-July P E-May	Tr L-Sept Tr L-Oct WR M-May Tr L-Sept	1.2 × 0.8 Pale brown or gray marked with brown, gray or black.	3-4
40	Herring Gull	DC M-Sept NY L-Aug StL M-Oct SF L-Oct	WR M-May WR L-May WR L-Apr WR M-Apr	2.9 × 1.9 Variable. Whitish to gray or brown; brown spots and blotches.	3-4

Nests		Food
Materials	**Location**	
Straw, grass, rushes; lined with down.	On dry ground in the open.	Rushes, pondweeds, seeds of aquatic plants; molluscs and insects.
Reeds, lined with down.	On ground in reeds or rushes, near water.	Wild celery, pondweeds and other aquatic plants; some molluscs, and aquatic insects.
Leaves, grasses, moss; lined with down.	On ground; beneath bushes and between boulders; or in a hole in a tree.	Fish, crayfish, frogs, occasional aquatic insects.
Heaps of reeds, rushes, and coarse grass.	On ground near water; sometimes half afloat.	Duckweeds and other aquatic plants. Molluscs, crustaceans, and aquatic insects.
Slight depression lined with pebbles, grasses, or debris.	A hollow in ground, in pastures or fields.	Mainly insects and earthworms; small crustaceans.
Slight depression lined with grass.	On ground or on slight elevation in meadows, open marshes, or bogs.	Insects, crustaceans, worms, seeds of swamp and aquatic plants.
Slight depression with little or no lining.	On ground along shores and in marshes, often under small bush.	Small fish, snails, worms, crustaceans, and some insects.
Slight depression lined with grasses.	On ground or cavity in rocks, on sandy or rocky shores. Banks of streams and open upland fields.	Mainly insects; worms, spiders, and small crustaceans.
Slight depression, sparingly lined with grass.	On ground or rock in grassy lowlands near water. Sometimes on moist upland.	Aquatic insects, worms, and small crustaceans.
Seaweeds; marsh plants, chips, feathers, shells. Sometimes no nest.	On ground. Birds nest in colonies. Often on islands; sometimes under heavy vegetation.	Small fish, molluscs, crustaceans, insects, garbage, blueberries.

Page	Name	Migration		Eggs	
		Arrive	Depart	Size (in.)	N
41	Common Tern	DC M-Apr NY L-Apr B E-May SF L-Apr	SR E-Oct SR E-Oct SR E-Oct Tr E-Nov	1.6 × 1.2 Variable. Dull greenis white to brown; dark spots.	2-
42	Turkey Vulture	DC Permanent Resident NY L-Mar SF E-Mar P M-Mar	 SR M-Nov SR M-Nov SR L-Sept	2.8 × 1.9 Dull white or buff; irreg ular brown spots.	1-
43	Osprey	DC L-Mar B L-Apr StL E-Apr SF M-Mar	SR M-Oct SR E-Oct Tr L-Oct SR M-Oct	2.5 × 1.8 Variable. Dull white buff or light brown wit brown blotches.	2-
44	Bald Eagle	DC Permanent Resident		3.5 × 2.9 White; unmarked.	1-
45	Cooper's Hawk	NY E-Apr B M-Apr StL M-Mar SF Permanent Resident	Tr E-Oct SR E-Oct SR L-Oct	1.9 × 1.6 Bluish or greenish whit unmarked to heavil spotted with brown.	3-
46	Red-tailed Hawk	Permanent Resident throughout its range, except in north central states		2.6 × 1.8 Dull or creamy white spotted brown or purpl rarely unmarked.	2-
47	American Kestrel	Permanent Resident throughout its range, except in north central states and Canada		1.3 × 1.2 White or tinted with buf spotted or speckled wit brown.	4-
48	Ring-necked Pheasant	Permanent Resident throughout its range		1.8 × 1.4 Buff to dark olive; occa sionally greenish.	6-1
49	Ruffed Grouse	Permanent Resident throughout its range		1.5 × 1.1 Pale buff but varying i color; unmarked.	8-1
50	Northern Bobwhite	Permanent Resident throughout its range		1.2 × 1.0 White; unmarked.	10-2

Nests		Food
Materials	**Location**	
Hollow, lined with shells, to well-built mound of grass and seaweed.	On sand or bare rock, sometimes among grasses. Usually on islands.	Feeds almost wholly on small fish, but also some insects.
None.	On ground, rock ledge, or hollow log in secluded places, near water or in woods.	Carrion.
Platform of sticks; additions made from year to year.	In trees: 15-50 ft. up or on rocks. Ospreys nest along coasts.	Almost entirely fish.
Large nest of branches and sticks. Additions and repairs are made yearly.	In treetops or cliffs; 30-90 ft. up; in forested or wooded regions, near streams, lakes, or ocean.	Mostly fish; some rodents and a few birds.
Branches and twigs; often lined with bark.	Usually in trees: pines preferred, 25-65 ft. up. Rarely on ground.	Mainly wild birds and poultry; some mammals; other vertebrates and insects.
Branches and twigs; lined with grasses, weeds, dead leaves.	In tall trees, 20-80 ft. up; in forest areas or in small groves.	Mainly rodents; some reptiles and poultry.
No nest material, unless some was left by previous occupant.	In cavity of tree, cliff embankment, 7-80 ft. up; often in farms or orchards.	Largely insects, some rodents, lizards, and small birds.
Dead leaves, grass, straw.	On ground in bushy pastures, moorlands, grass, and grain fields.	Corn, wheat, barley, wild fruits, and insects.
Shallow depression, lined with leaves.	On ground, at base of tree in wooded uplands or dense thicket; under logs.	Leaves, buds, and fruits of forest plants. Occasional insects.
Grass, stems, strips of bark.	On ground in grass tangles, open fields, hedgerows.	Corn and grain. Ragweed, lespedeza, acorns, and weed seeds.

Page	Name	Migration		Eggs	
		Arrive	Depart	Size (in.)	No.
51	Rock Dove	Permanent Resident throughout its range		1.5 × 1.1 White; unmarked.	2-3
52	Mourning Dove	DC Permanent Resident NY M-Mar B L-Mar SF L-Mar	SR M-Nov SR L-Oct SR M-Nov	1.1 × 0.8 White; unmarked.	2
53	Yellow-billed Cuckoo	DC E-May NY E-May StL L-Apr SF L-May	SR L-Sept SR L-Sept SR L-Sept SR L-Sept	1.2 × 0.9 Light bluish green; unmarked; occasionally mottled.	2-4
54	Common Barn-Owl	Permanent Resident except at northern edge of its range		1.6 × 1.2 White; unmarked.	5-11
55	Great Horned Owl	Permanent Resident throughout its range		2.3 × 1.9 Rough white; unmarked.	2-3
56	Eastern and Western Screech-Owls	Permanent Residents throughout their range		1.4 × 1.3 White; unmarked.	3-5
57	Chimney Swift	DC M-Apr B L-Apr StL E-Apr	SR E-Oct SR E-Sept SR E-Oct	0.8 × 0.5 White; unmarked.	4-5
58	Whip-poor-will	DC L-Apr B E-May StL M-Apr	SR M-Sept SR M-Sept SR M-Oct	1.2 × 0.8 Creamy white; spotted with brown.	2
59	Common Nighthawk	DC E-May B M-May StL L-Apr P E-June	SR L-Sept SR M-Sept SR E-Oct SR L-Sept	1.2 × 0.9 Dull white; spotted with gray and brown.	2
60	Ruby-throated Hummingbird	DC L-Apr NY M-May StL L-Apr	SR L-Sept SR M-Sept SR E-Oct	0.5 × 0.4 White; unmarked.	2

Nests		Food
Materials	**Location**	
Sticks, straw, and debris.	Building (30 ft. and higher), on sheltered eaves or ledge.	Corn, oats, weed seeds, farm gleanings.
Stems, straws, sometimes leaves and moss.	In trees (pines preferred) 2-45 ft. above ground; in upland, sometimes in wet lowlands.	Wheat, corn, grass, and weed seeds.
Sticks, rootlets, straws, pine needles, lichens.	In trees or thickets, 3-20 ft. up. Prefers margins of woods, orchards, or thickets.	Insects, mostly caterpillars, including hairy species.
Sometimes rubbish or debris. Usually no nest.	Tree cavities; steeples, barns. Sometimes underground in burrows or holes in embankments.	Mice, rats, gophers, and some birds.
Sometimes uses old hawk nests; sometimes none.	In large trees (preferably pines) 10-90 ft. up. Sometimes in tree hollow or even on ground.	Rabbits, squirrels, rats, wild birds and poultry.
No nest; or uses any available material.	Hollow of tree (5-50 ft. up), cranny, nook of building.	Rodents, small birds, frogs, fish, and insects.
Coarse twigs, held together by saliva of bird.	Usually near top of chimneys or rarely in barns or sheds; sometimes inside wells.	Flies, mosquitoes, and other small insects, caught in flight.
No nest construction. Uses slight depression in leaves.	On ground, usually in brushy wood margins, on well-drained land.	Moths, flying ants, and other insects caught in flight.
None. Eggs laid on bare surface.	On ground, rock, or on flat roofs of building; in open fields, pastures, or city lots.	Similar to Whip-poor-will.
Plant-down, bits of lichen outside; bound by threads of saliva and spider web.	Placed or "saddled" on branch of tree—3-50 ft. above ground.	Nectar of flowers and small insects.

Page	Name	Migration		Eggs	
		Arrive	Depart	Size (in.)	N
61	Belted Kingfisher	DC Permanent Resident B E-Apr SR L-Oct StL L-Feb SR L-Nov SF Permanent Resident		1.3 × 1.0 Glossy white; unmarked	5-
62	Red-headed Woodpecker	DC Permanent Resident NY M-May Tr L-Sept StL Permanent Resident		1.0 × 0.8 White; unmarked.	4-
63	Northern Flicker	DC Permanent Resident NY M-Mar SR L-Oct B M-Apr SR M-Oct SF Permanent Resident		1.1 × 0.9 Glossy white; unmarked	5-
64	Yellow-bellied Sapsucker	DC L-Sept WR E-May B M-Apr Tr L-Oct StL E-Mar Tr M-Nov SF E-Oct WR L-Apr		0.9 × 0.7 Glossy white; unmarked	5-
65	Downy Woodpecker	Permanent Resident throughout its range		0.8 × 0.6 White; unmarked.	4-
66	Eastern Kingbird	DC L-Apr SR M-Sept NY E-May SR E-Sept StL L-Apr SR L-Sept P M-May SR M-Sept		1.0 × 0.7 Creamy white, spotted with brown.	3-
67	Great Crested Flycatcher	DC E-May SR M-Sept B M-May SR E-Sept StL L-Apr SR M-Sept		0.9 × 0.7 Creamy, streaked with brown.	3-
68	Eastern Phoebe	DC M-Mar SR L-Oct NY M-Mar SR M-Oct StL M-Mar SR L-Oct		0.8 × 0.6 White; occasionally spot- ted with brown.	4-
69	Least Flycatcher	DC E-May Tr L-Sept B E-May SR E-Sept StL E-May Tr E-Oct		0.6 × 0.5 White; unmarked.	3-
70	Horned Lark	Permanent Resident in the United States		0.8 × 0.6 Dull white; speckled with brown or purple.	3-

Nests		Food
Materials	Location	
Nest lined with fish-bones and scales, leaves, grass.	At end of burrow in bank or bluff. Usually not more than 10 ft. up. Usually near water.	Mainly fish; some crustaceans and frogs.
A gourd-shaped hole, padded with chips.	Excavations in trees, posts, poles: 5-80 ft. up.	Beetles, ants, other insects. Acorns, other wild fruits and seeds.
Hole, padded with chips.	Cavity 10-24 in. deep in trees, snags, poles: 6 in.-60 ft. up.	Ants, beetles, and other insects. Wild fruits and seeds.
Hole, lined with chips.	Cavity in dead or live tree 8-40 ft. up; in woods or orchards.	Ants, beetles, other insects and their eggs. Wood and sap; wild fruits.
Gourd-shaped excavation: 6-10 in. deep.	In dead limb 5-50 ft. up; woodlands, orchards.	Ants and boring insects, spiders, snails. Some fruits and seeds.
Rootlets, grass, twine, hair, wool. Lined with fine grass, moss.	On horizontal limb of tree; bushes, eaves, fence rails, bridges: 2-60 ft. up.	Bees, ants, grasshoppers, beetles, etc. Also some wild fruits.
Twigs, grass, leaves, moss, feathers, and usually a cast-off snakeskin.	Cavity in dead limb or post. Sometimes buildings; 3-70 ft. up.	Moths, grasshoppers, other flying insects. Occasional fruits.
Of mud, covered with moss and dead leaves, lined with grass rootlets, moss, feathers.	In shelter of undercut banks, tree roots, culverts, eaves, or inside farm buildings; 1-20 ft up.	Flying insects: beetles, flies, moths, etc. Some wild fruit; few seeds.
Grasses, bark fibers, lined with feathers and other soft materials.	Fork of tree or upright twigs: 2-60 ft. up. Usually along wood margins.	Small insects: flies, mosquitoes, moths, beetles.
Depression, loosely filled with grass, fibers, feathers.	On ground, in cultivated fields, sand dunes, or barren islands; in cover of grass and moss.	Mixed diet of insects and (in winter) seeds of weeds and grasses.

Page	Name	Migration		Eggs	
		Arrive	Depart	Size (in.)	No.
71	Purple Martin	DC L-Mar NY M-Apr StL L-Mar	SR E-Sept Tr L-Aug SR M-Sept	1.0×0.7 White; unmarked.	4-5
72	Tree Swallow	DC L-Mar B M-Apr StL M-Mar SF E-Mar	Tr M-Oct SR M-Sept SR L-Oct SR L-Oct	0.7×0.6 White; unmarked.	4-7
73	Barn Swallow	NY E-Apr StL E-Apr SF L-Mar P M-Apr	SR L-Sept SR L-Oct SR M-Oct SR M-Sept	0.8×0.5 White, spotted with brown.	3-6
74	Black-billed Magpie	Permanent Resident throughout its range		1.3×0.9 Grayish, heavily marked with brown.	4-8
75	American Crow	Permanent Resident except in Canada		1.6×1.2 Variable. Pale greenish or bluish, spotted or blotched with brown.	3-5
76	Blue Jay	Permanent Resident throughout its range but irregular in winter in the north		1.1×0.9 Greenish to olive, spotted with brown.	4-6
77	White-breasted Nuthatch	Permanent Resident throughout its range		0.8×0.6 White, rarely pinkish; speckled or spotted with brown.	5-8
78	Black-capped Chickadee	Permanent Resident throughout its range		0.6×0.5 White, finely spotted with brown.	5-8
79	Tufted Titmouse	Permanent Resident throughout its range		0.7×0.6 White to buff; speckled with grayish brown.	5-8
80	Brown Creeper	DC E-Oct NY L-Sept StL L-Sept SF Permanent Resident	WR L-Apr WR E-May WR L-Apr	0.6×0.5 White, speckled with brown.	5-8

Nests		Food
Materials	**Location**	
Leaves, grass, straw, twigs.	In cavities of trees, holes in cliffs: 3-30 ft. high. Frequently uses multi-celled birdhouses.	Flying insects: flies, bees, beetles, flying ants, moths.
Grass, lining of feathers.	Hollows and cavities in trees, woodpecker holes, crevices in buildings; also birdhouses; 2-50 ft. up.	Flies, moths, bees, beetles and other flying insects. Uses bayberries as a winter food.
Mud reinforced with plant material. Lined with feathers.	Commonly in barns, out-buildings, porches; 5-20 ft. up. Nest adheres to an upright surface.	Entirely flying insects: flies, bees, ants, beetles.
Large nest of sticks and mud; lining of rootlets or horsehair.	In bushes and trees: 8-30 ft. up.	Grasshoppers; other insects, carrion, small mammals; wild and cultivated fruits.
Twigs and sticks, lined with rootlets, vines, grass.	In trees (preferably pine woods), height 10-70 ft.	Corn and other grains, weed seeds, wild fruits; grasshoppers and other insects.
Twigs and rootlets, lined with grass, feathers.	In a fork of tree: 5-50 ft. up. Prefers evergreen forests. But often in suburbs, farms, and villages.	Acorns, beechnuts, corn and other grain. Some insects, eggs, and young birds.
Grass, plant fibers, twigs, hair, and feathers.	A cavity or deserted woodpecker hole: 5-60 ft. up. Mature trees preferred.	Beetles, ants, other insects and their eggs. Also seeds in winter. Prefers sunflower seeds.
Moss, hair, feathers, grass; lined with plant down.	Cavity in rotted stump or limb, or deserted woodpecker hole; 1-50 ft. up.	Insects and their eggs, weed and tree seeds; wild fruits.
Leaves, moss, bark; lined with feathers.	Deserted woodpeckers' holes or stumps: 2-85 ft. up.	Ants, bugs, and other insects; some seeds and fruits.
Twigs, plant fibers; sometimes lined with spider web, feathers, or hair.	In trees, behind or between loose bark: 5-15 ft. up. Usually in deep woods.	Mainly insects: beetles, bugs, caterpillars, ants, insect eggs.

Page	Name	Migration		Eggs	
		Arrive	Depart	Size (in.)	No.
81	House Wren	DC M-Apr NY L-Apr StL M-Apr SF E-Mar	SR M-Oct SR E-Oct SR M-Oct SR L-Oct	0.7 × 0.5 Dull white, densely spot- ted with brown.	5-10
82	Ruby-crowned Kinglet	NY E-Apr B M-Apr StL E-Oct P M-Apr	Tr L-Oct Tr M-Oct Tr L-Apr SR M-Oct	0.5 × 0.4 White to cream. Similar to Golden-crowned King- let.	4-9
83	Golden-crowned Kinglet	DC E-Oct NY L-Sept StL L-Sept SF Permanent Resident	WR M-Apr WR M-Apr WR L-Apr	0.6 × 0.4 White to cream; spotted with pale brown.	5-10
84	Blue-gray Gnatcatcher	DC M-Apr NY L-Apr StL L-Mar SF Permanent Resident	SR M-Sept SR E-Sept SR L-Sept	0.6 × 0.5 White or bluish white; speckled with brown.	4-5
85	Eastern Bluebird	DC Permanent Resident NY M-Mar StL L-Feb P Permanent Resident	SR M-Nov SR L-Nov	0.9 × 0.7 Pale blue; rarely white; unmarked.	4-6
86	Wood Thrush	DC L-Apr NY E-May B M-May StL L-Apr	SR M-Oct SR E-Oct SR M-Sept SR E-Oct	1.1 × 0.8 Bright greenish blue; un- marked.	3-5
87	Hermit Thrush	DC M-Oct NY E-Apr B M-Apr SF Permanent Resident	WR E-May SR M-Nov SR E-Nov	0.9 × 0.7 Greenish blue; un- marked.	3-4
88	American Robin	DC Permanent Resident NY E-Mar StL Permanent Resident SF Permanent Resident	SR M-Nov	1.2 × 0.8 Greenish blue; rarely spotted.	3-5
89	Gray Catbird	DC L-Apr NY E-May StL L-Apr	SR L-Oct SR E-Oct SR M-Oct	0.9 × 0.7 Deep greenish blue or bluish green; unmarked.	4-6
90	Northern Mockingbird	DC Permanent Resident StL Permanent Resident SF Permanent Resident		1.0 × 0.8 Greenish to blue; spotted brown, mostly at large end.	3-6

Nests		Food
Materials	**Location**	
Twigs, stems, grasses, lined with feathers, hair.	A cavity in hollow tree: 5-60 ft. up. Woodlands, farmyards, and in cities. Bird boxes commonly used.	Small insects: bugs, beetles, caterpillars, etc.
Plant down, covered by mosses and lichens. Bound with plant fibers.	In conifers, often saddled on a limb; 5-50 ft. up.	Ants, plant lice, scale insects, and insect eggs. Occasional use of wild fruits.
Green mosses, lined with fine inner bark, black rootlets, and feathers.	In coniferous trees, partly suspended from twigs: 4-60 ft. up.	Insects: flies, beetles, plant lice; insect eggs.
Tendrils, fine bark, and grasses. Firmly woven and covered with lichens.	On a branch or in a crotch in tree near water; 10-70 ft. up.	Mainly small insects: beetles, flies, caterpillars, moths.
Grasses, rootlets, hair, and some feathers.	In hollow trees, deserted woodpecker holes, and birdhouses; 3-30 ft. up.	Many insects, including beetles, weevils, and grasshoppers. Also holly, dogwood, and other wild fruits.
Leaves, rootlets, fine twigs. Firmly woven, with inner wall of mud.	Usually in saplings in woods; 3-40 ft. up.	Beetles, ants, caterpillars, and other insects. Some wild fruits and weed seeds.
Moss, grasses, leaves. Lined with rootlets and pine needles.	On or near ground in pine or hemlock woods.	Food similar to Wood Thrush.
Mud wall and bottom, reinforced with grass, twine, twigs. Lined with grass.	In tree crotch or among branches, 5-70 ft. up. In woods or open country. On buildings, in rural areas.	Garden and field insects, worms; cultivated and wild fruits. Some seeds.
Twigs and leaves. Lined with bark shreds, rootlets.	In shrubbery, thicket; 1-10 ft. and rarely 25 ft. up. Prefers dense lowlands.	Food similar to Mockingbird.
Bulky nest of coarse twigs, weed stems, shreds, string, rags.	In shrubs, thickets, vines; near houses; 1-15 ft. up, rarely higher.	Beetles, grasshoppers, and other insects; some wild fruit in season—grape and holly preferred.

Page	Name	Migration		Eggs	
		Arrive	Depart	Size (in.)	No.
91	Brown Thrasher	DC E-Apr NY L-Apr B L-Apr StL M-Mar	SR M-Oct SR M-Oct SR M-Sept SR M-Nov	1.1 × 0.8 3-6 Grayish or greenish white; thickly spotted with brown.	
92	Cedar Waxwing	DC E-Sept NY M-May StL L-Sept P Permanent Resident	WR E-June SR M-Nov WR M-June	0.9 × 0.6 3-5 Grayish blue; speckled brown or black, mostly at large end.	
93	Loggerhead Shrike	NY E-Aug B M-Mar StL Permanent Resident SF Permanent Resident	Tr L-Oct Tr L-Oct	1.0 × 0.8 3-5 Dull white; spotted and blotched with light brown.	
94	European Starling	Permanent Resident throughout its range, except in extreme North		1.2 × 0.9 4-6 Whitish or pale blue; unmarked.	
96	Yellow Warbler	DC L-Apr NY E-May StL L-Apr SF M-Apr	SR M-Sept SR L-Aug SR M-Sept SR L-Sept	0.7 × 0.5 4-5 Pale bluish white; brown spots forming ring at larger end.	
96	Black-and-white Warbler	DC M-Apr NY L-Apr StL M-Apr	SR E-Oct SR M-Sept SR L-Sept	0.7 × 0.5 4-5 Greenish white to buff; spotted and blotched with brown.	
96	Black-throated Blue Warbler	DC E-May NY E-May B M-May StL E-May	Tr E-Oct Tr L-Sept Tr M-Sept Tr M-Sept	0.7 × 0.5 3-5 Creamy white; speckled with brown and lavender, mostly at larger end.	
98	Common Yellowthroat	DC L-Apr NY E-May StL E-Apr SF Permanent Resident	SR M-Oct SR M-Oct SR E-Oct	0.7 × 0.5 3-5 Creamy white; speckled with brown and black; chiefly at large end.	
98	Ovenbird	DC L-Apr NY E-May StL L-Apr	SR E-Oct SR M-Sept SR E-Oct	0.8 × 0.6 4-6 White, spotted with brown, especially at larger end.	
98	Northern Waterthrush	DC L-Apr B M-May StL L-Apr	Tr L-Sept Tr E-Sept Tr L-Sept	0.8 × 0.6 4-5 White to creamy; spotted with brown and gray.	

Nests		Food
Materials	**Location**	
Bulky nest of coarse twigs, weed stalks, leaves. Lined with rootlets, grass.	In bushes, vines, brush, and low trees; 0-12 ft. up.	Beetles, grasshoppers, caterpillars, etc. Also some acorns and wild fruit.
Bulky nest of bark, leaves, grasses, rootlets, moss, and sometimes mud.	Often in fruit and shade trees; 5-50 ft. up.	Wild and cultivated fruits: grapes, dogwood, hawthorn, cherries; some insects.
Strips of bark, small twigs, and vegetable fibers; lined with grasses.	In thorny hedges or low trees; 5-20 ft. up.	Insects; grasshoppers, beetles; some small rodents and birds.
Large, poorly built nest of grasses and twigs.	In hollow of tree or crevice of building; 3-40 ft. up. Uses bird boxes.	Beetles, grasshoppers, and other insects; wild and cultivated fruits and grain.
Fine grasses and fibers; lined with plant down, fine grass, some hair.	In shrubs and trees; 3-8 ft. up. Rarely 40 ft. Fields and orchards, near water.	Caterpillars, weevils, and other small insects. Slight amount of plant food.
Strips of fine bark, grasses; lined with rootlets or hairs.	On ground, at base of trees, logs, or rocks.	Plant lice, caterpillars, beetles, scale and other insects.
Bark, fine grasses, pine needles. Lining of black rootlets.	In heavy undergrowth of dense woods; 1-10 ft. up.	Mainly insects: caterpillars, small beetles, plant lice, etc.
Bark, coarse grasses, dead leaves. Lined with fine grass tendrils.	On or near ground. Usually in clump of grass, in moist location.	Insects: cankerworms, weevils, leafhoppers, caterpillars, etc.
Bulky, covered nest. Entrance at one side. Of leaves, coarse grasses, and rootlets.	On leaf-covered ground in open woods.	Beetles, grasshoppers, and other ground insects. Worms and spiders.
Moss, lined with tendrils and fine rootlets.	On ground in a mossy bank or under roots of fallen tree.	Insects: beetles, bugs, caterpillars, leafhoppers, and spiders.

Page	Name	Migration		Eggs	
		Arrive	Depart	Size (in.)	No.
100	Yellow-rumped Warbler	DC L-Sept NY L-Sept StL M-Sept SF L-Sept	WR M-May WR E-May WR M-May WR L-Apr	0.7 × 0.5 4-5 White, speckled with brown; often forming ring at larger end.	
100	American Redstart	DC L-Apr B E-May StL M-Apr	SR E-Oct SR M-Sept SR L-Sept	0.7 × 0.5 4-5 Bluish white; brown spots occasionally ringing large end.	
100	Wilson's Warbler	DC E-May NY M-May StL E-May SF L-Mar	Tr L-Sept Tr M-Sept Tr M-Sept SR L-Sept	0.7 × 0.5 4-5 White or pinkish; brown spots forming ring at larger end.	
102	Red-eyed Vireo	DC E-May B M-May StL M-Apr P E-May	SR E-Oct SR M-Sept SR E-Oct SR L-Sept	0.9 × 0.6 3-4 White, sparsely speckled with brown or black.	
103	Scarlet Tanager	DC L-Apr B M-May StL L-Apr	SR E-Oct SR M-Sept SR E-Oct	0.9 × 0.7 3-4 Pale greenish or bluish; speckled brown at larger end.	
104	Northern Cardinal	Permanent Resident		1.0 × 0.7 3-4 Pale bluish white; finely spotted with reddish brown.	
105	Rose-breasted Grosbeak	DC E-May NY M-May StL L-Apr	Tr E-Oct SR M-Sept SR E-Oct	0.9 × 0.7 4-5 Pale blue; spotted with brown.	
106	Indigo Bunting	DC L-Apr B M-May StL L-Apr	SR E-Oct SR M-Sept SR L-Oct	0.7 × 0.6 3-4 Pale bluish white; unmarked.	
107	Rufous-sided Towhee	NY M-Apr B L-Apr StL E-Mar	SR E-Oct SR E-Oct SR L-Nov	1.0 × 0.7 4-5 White or pinkish; brown specks at large end.	
108	Brown Towhee	Permanent Resident		1.0 × 0.7 3-4 Variable; bluish marked with purple and black.	

Nests		Food
Materials	**Location**	
Plant fibers; lining of grasses.	Coniferous trees in heavy woods; 5-40 ft. up.	Mainly common insects, but takes poison ivy, bayberry, and other fruits in winter.
Bark, leafstalks, plant down. Firmly woven and lined with rootlets.	Usually in the crotch of a sapling; 3-30 ft. above ground, rarely higher.	Small insects: flies, beetles, moths, leafhoppers, etc.
Ball of grass and moss wrapped in leaves. Lined with fine rootlets.	On ground among bushes in swampy land.	Small insects, similar to other warblers. Makes slight use of plant food.
Strips of bark, paper, plant down. Firmly and smoothly woven. Lined with bark and tendrils.	Suspended from a forked branch; 3-75 ft. up.	Caterpillars, moths, bugs, beetles, and other insects; small amount of wild fruit.
Fine twigs and weeds. Lined with vine tendrils and stems.	On horizontal limb, often near its end; 10-70 ft. up.	Mainly insects: ants, beetles, moths, caterpillars. Dogwood, blackberry, and other wild fruits.
Twigs, rootlets, strips of bark. Lined with grasses and rootlets.	In thick bushes or vines; 2-10 ft. up. Rarely up to 30 ft.	Grape, holly, blackberry; wild seeds and a good many kinds of insects.
Loose nest of fine twigs, weeds, rootlets.	In trees or bushes; 5-20 ft. up.	Insects, including beetles, caterpillars, ants, bees. Wild fruits when available.
Grasses, bits of dead leaves, bark; lined with fine grass, rootlets, hairs.	In crotch of bush or sapling; 1-10 ft. up. Rarely as high as 20 ft.	Diet mixed: caterpillars and other insects; some wild fruits, weed seeds.
Dead leaves and bark; lined with fine grasses.	Usually on ground, sometimes in bushes or saplings; 0-10 ft. up.	Wild fruits and weed seeds. Insects, worms, and spiders.
Grasses, weeds, and twigs. Lined with rootlets.	On ground or in low bushes. Less than 10 ft. up.	Oats and barley; weed seeds, caterpillars and other insects.

Page	Name	Migration		Eggs	
		Arrive	Depart	Size (in.)	No
110	Field Sparrow	NY M-Apr B M-Apr StL E-Mar	SR L-Oct SR M-Oct SR L-Nov	0.7 × 0.5	3- White to pale blue o green; speckled wit brown.
110	American Tree Sparrow	NY M-Nov B L-Oct StL M-Nov P L-Oct	WR L-Mar WR E-Apr WR L-Mar WR M-Mar	0.8 × 0.6	4- Pale greenish or bluish green; speckled with ligh brown.
110	Vesper Sparrow	DC E-Apr B M-Apr StL M-Mar P E-Apr	SR L-Oct SR M-Oct Tr E-Nov SR M-Sept	0.9 × 0.6	4- Dull white; thickly spot ted with brown.
112	Chipping Sparrow	DC L-Mar B M-Apr StL L-Mar SF M-Apr	SR E-Nov SR M-Oct SR L-Oct SR M-Oct	0.7 × 0.5	4- Greenish blue; speckle with brown, mostly o larger end.
112	White-crowned Sparrow	DC E-May NY M-May StL M-Apr SF Permanent Resident	Tr M-Nov Tr L-Oct Tr L-Nov	0.9 × 0.6	4- Bluish and greenis white, spotted wit brown.
112	White-throated Sparrow	DC L-Sept NY L-Sept StL E-Oct	WR M-May Tr M-May Tr M-May	0.8 × 0.6	4- White to bluish; speckle and blotched with red dish brown.
114	Song Sparrow	Permanent Resident over much of its range		0.8 × 0.6	4- Variable. White or green ish; spotted and speckle with brown.
114	Swamp Sparrow	DC E-Oct B M-Apr StL E-Oct	WR E-May SR M-Oct WR L-Apr	0.8 × 0.6	4- Bluish white; spotted blotched with brown.
114	Fox Sparrow	DC L-Oct NY M-Oct StL E-Oct SF E-Oct	Tr E-Apr Tr M-Apr Tr M-Apr WR L-Apr	0.8 × 0.6	4- Greenish white; spotte with dull brown.
116	Dark-eyed Junco	DC E-Oct NY L-Sept StL E-Oct P E-Oct	WR E-May WR M-May WR L-Apr WR M-Mar	0.8 × 0.6	4 Pale bluish white; brow spots may form ring larger end.

Nests		Food
Materials	Location	
Coarse grasses, weeds, rootlets. Lined with fine grass and hairs.	On ground or low bushes (10 ft. or less) in fields, overgrown pastures.	Similar to American Tree Sparrow, with some use of grain.
Grasses, rootlets, and hair.	On ground or in stunted conifers near timberline; near water.	Largely weed seeds; crabgrass, pigweed, sedge, etc. Some insects eaten.
Coarse grass. Lined with finer grasses, rootlets, hairs.	On ground in dry upland fields; along dry roadsides.	Weed seeds of many kinds; some grain, and various insects.
Grasses, fine twigs, rootlets. Thickly lined with hair.	In trees or bushes; in shrubbery near houses; 3-35 ft. up. Rarely on ground.	Weed seeds, oats, and timothy; leafhoppers and other common insects.
Grasses, moss, and rootlets. Lined with hair.	Usually on ground or in clump of grass in woods or thickets.	Ragweed, pigweed, knotweed, and other weed seeds; some grain and a number of kinds of insects.
Grasses, rootlets, moss, strips of bark. Lined with finer grasses.	Usually on ground in hedgerows and woodland undergrowth.	Food very similar to that of White-crowned Sparrow.
Nest of grasses and rootlets. Lined with fine grasses and hair.	On ground or in low bushes; in grass thickets or saplings. Up to 8 ft.; rarely 15 ft.	Food similar to that of Swamp Sparrow.
Coarse grasses, rootlets, dead leaves. Lined with finer grasses and sometimes hair.	On or close to ground; in grasses in wet meadows, marshes or swamps.	Seeds of weeds and grasses. Beetles, caterpillars, and other insects.
Coarse grasses. Lined with finer grasses, hair, mosses, feathers.	On ground or in low bushes; coniferous forests or alder thickets preferred.	Weed seeds, wild fruits, some grain, millipedes, and various insects.
Grasses, moss, and rootlets. Lined with fine grass and hair.	On or very near ground in fallen tree, logs, upturned roots; under overhanging banks, along wood roads.	Ragweed, crabgrass, and other weed seeds. Some caterpillars and other insects.

Page	Name	Migration		Eggs	N
		Arrive	Depart	Size (in.)	
117	Eastern Meadowlark	DC Permanent Resident NY M-Mar SR L-Oct B L-Mar SR L-Oct StL Permanent Resident		1.1×0.8 White; completely spo[t]ted and speckled wi[th] brown.	3
118	Bobolink	DC E-May Tr L-Sept B M-May SR M-Sept StL E-May Tr L-May P L-May SR M-Sept		0.9×0.6 Dull white; spotted a[nd] blotched with brown a[nd] gray.	4
119	Red-winged Blackbird	DC M-Feb SR M-Nov NY M-Mar SR L-Oct StL E-Mar SR E-Nov SF Permanent Resident		1.0×0.7 Bluish white; irregu[lar] spots and streaks of p[ur]ple and black.	3
120	Brewer's Blackbird	StL M-Mar Tr E-Apr SF Permanent Resident P Permanent Resident		1.0×0.8 Dull white; almost e[n]tirely spotted with bro[wn] and black.	4
121	Common Grackle	DC M-Feb SR L-Nov NY E-Mar SR E-Nov StL Permanent Resident		1.2×0.8 Bluish white; speckl[ed] and spotted dark bro[wn] to black.	3
122	Brown-headed Cowbird	DC E-Mar SR E-Nov NY M-Mar SR M-Oct StL E-Mar SR L-Nov P E-May SR L-Sept		0.9×0.7 White or bluish; heav[ily] speckled with gray [or] brown.	4
123	Northern Oriole	DC L-Apr Tr L-Sept NY M-May SR E-Sept StL M-Apr SR E-Sept		0.9×0.6 White; irregular strea[ks] and blotches of brown a[nd] black.	4
124	Purple Finch	DC E-Oct WR E-May NY L-Mar Tr E-Nov StL E-Oct WR L-Apr SF Permanent Resident		0.8×0.6 Blue; spotted and spe[ck]led with brown at larg[e] end.	4
125	House Finch	Permanent Resident		0.8×0.6 Pale blue, nearly whi[te] thinly speckled wi[th] black.	3
126	American Goldfinch	Permanent Resident		0.7×0.5 Pale bluish white; u[n]marked.	3
127	House Sparrow	Permanent Resident throughout its range		0.9×0.6 White to dull bro[wn] speckled with brown.	4

Nests		Food
Materials	**Location**	
Grasses and weeds; often arched over.	Usually on ground in grassy fields or meadows.	Grain and wild grass seeds, wild fruits, grasshoppers, and other insects.
Nest of grasses, weed stems, and rootlets.	On ground in the tall meadow grasses.	Wild rice, cultivated grains, weed seeds, caterpillars and other insects.
Coarse grasses and weeds. Lined with finer grass and rootlets.	Attached to low bushes, reeds; usually in swamps. Usually less than 15 ft. up.	Weed and marsh plant seeds; grain; some fruit and insects in season.
Twigs and coarse grass. Lined with finer grass.	On ground or in shrubs or coniferous trees; 0-10 ft. up.	Oats and other grain, weed seeds, some insects.
Bulky, but compact. Of mud and coarse grasses; lined with finer grasses.	Nests in colonies, most often in coniferous trees; sometimes in bushes; 5-80 ft. up.	Grain and weed seeds. Some wild fruit; beetles, grasshoppers, crickets, etc.
None added.	Eggs laid in nests of other birds. Usually 1 or 2 in any one nest.	Grain and weed seeds. Grasshoppers and other insects.
Grasses, plant fibers, hair, string, etc. Firmly interwoven.	Hanging from end of branches in shade or fruit trees; 10-90 ft. up.	Caterpillars, beetles, and other insects; wild and some cultivated fruits.
Twigs, grasses, and rootlets. Thickly lined with hairs.	Woods, in pine and spruce trees; 5-60 ft. up.	Tree seeds and wild fruits. Some insects.
Rootlets and grasses. Lined with horsehair.	Trees, bushes, and vines; 5-20 ft. above ground. Often on or near buildings.	Weed seeds, tree seeds, plant lice and other insects.
Fine grasses, bark, moss; thickly lined with thistledown.	In trees or bushes; 5-35 ft. up.	Mainly weed seeds, grain, and wild fruit. Occasional plant lice and caterpillars.
Of any available material: string, straw, twigs, paper, etc.	In any available place: in buildings, structures, eaves; over 5 ft. up.	Corn, oats, wheat, and other grain; weed seeds; some insects during spring and summer.

BIRDING AIDS

PUBLICATIONS Here are a few of the best publications to start you on more advanced bird study:

Robbins, C. S., B. Bruun, and H. S. Zim, **Birds of North America,** A Guide to Field Identification, Golden Press, N.Y., rev. ed., 1983.

Peterson, R. T., **A Field Guide to the Birds of Eastern and Central North America,** 4th ed., 1980; **A Field Guide to Western Birds,** 1961. Both Houghton Mifflin, Boston.

Pettingill, O. S., Jr., **A Guide to Bird Finding East of the Mississippi,** 2nd ed., 1977. **A Guide to Bird Finding West of the Mississippi,** rev. ed., 1981. Both Oxford Univ. Press, N.Y.

Pasquier, R. F., **Watching Birds**—An Introduction to Ornithology, Houghton Mifflin, Boston, 1977.

Rickert, J. E., **A Guide to North American Bird Clubs,** Avian Publications, P.O. Box 310, Elizabethtown, Ky. 42701.

Dennis, J. W., **A Complete Guide to Bird Feeding,** Knopf, N.Y., 1975.

Martin, A. C., H. S. Zim, and A. L. Nelson, **American Wildlife and Plants,** Dover, N.Y., 1961.

American Birds magazine, published by the National Audubon Society, 950 Third Ave., New York, N.Y. 10022.

MUSEUMS AND ZOOS are good places to supplement your field study.

Albany: New York State Museum

Atlanta: Georgia State Museum

Cambridge, Mass.: Museum of Comparative Zoology, Harvard Univ.

Chicago: Field Museum of Natural History; Brookfield Zoo

Denver: Denver Museum of Natural History

Gainesville, Fla.: Florida State Museum

Los Angeles: Los Angeles County Museum; Griffith Park (Zoo)

New Orleans: Louisiana State Museum; Audubon Park (Zoo)

New York: American Museum of Natural History; N.Y. Zoological Park

Philadelphia: Philadelphia Academy of Natural Sciences; Philadelphia Zoological Gardens

San Francisco: California Academy of Sciences; San Francisco Zoological Gardens

Seattle: Washington State Museum

Washington, D.C.: National Museum of Natural History; National Zoological Park

PLACES FOR STUDYING BIRDS

These National Wildlife Refuges (NWR), National Parks (NP), and other areas are famous for number and variety of birds.

Greater Roadrunner (22 in.), a long-tailed desert bird, rarely flies.

UNITED STATES

Alabama: Dauphin Island. **Arizona:** Huachuca Mts., Tombstone. **Arkansas:** White River NWR, St. Charles. **California:** Tule-Klamath Basin, Tulelake; Sacramento NWR, Willows; Yosemite NP. **Colorado:** Rocky Mt. NP. **Connecticut:** Audubon Nature Center, Greenwich. **Delaware:** Bombay Hook NWR, Smyrna. **Florida:** Everglades NP., Homestead; St. Marks NWR, St. Marks. **Georgia:** Okefenokee NWR, Folkston. **Illinois:** Chautauqua NWR, Havana. **Kansas:** Cheyenne Bottoms, Great Bend. **Louisiana:** Sabine NWR, Hackberry. **Maryland:** Ocean City; Pocomoke River Swamp, Powellsville. **Massachusetts:** Parker River NWR, Newburyport; Monomoy NWR, South Chatham. **Michigan:** Seney NWR, Seney. **Minnesota:** Itasca State Pk. **Mississippi:** Noxubee NWR, Brooksville. **Montana:** Red Rock Lakes NWR, Lima. **Nebraska:** Valentine NWR, Valentine. **New Hampshire:** Connecticut Lakes, Pittsburg. **New Jersey:** Cape May Point, Cape May; Brigantine NWR, Oceanville. **New Mexico:** Bosque del Apache NWR, Socorro. **New York:** Montauk Pt. State Pk., Montauk. **North Carolina:** Mattamuskeet NWR, Swan Quarter; Greenfield Pk., Wilmington. **North Dakota:** Des Lacs NWR, Kenmare. **Ohio:** Buckeye Lake, Hebron. **Oklahoma:** Wichita Mts. NWR, Indiahoma. **Oregon:** Malheur NWR, Princeton; Netarts Bay, Netarts. **Pennsylvania:** Hawk Mt., Kempton. **Rhode Island:** Sakonnet Pt., Little Compton. **South Carolina:** Cape Romain NWR, Awendaw. **South Dakota:** Sand Lake NWR, Columbia; Black Hills. **Tennessee:** Great Smoky Mts. NP, Gatlinburg; Reelfoot NWR, Union City. **Texas:** Santa Ana NWR, Alamo; Laguna Atascosa NWR, Rio Hondo; Rockport; Guadalupe Mts. NWR. **Vermont:** Missisquoi NWR, Swanton. **Virginia:** Back Bay NWR, Virginia Beach; Chincoteague NWR, Chincoteague; Dismal Swamp NWR, Suffolk. **Washington:** Willapa Bay area, Westport; Olympic NP; Mt. Rainier NP. **Wisconsin:** Horicon NWR, Mayville. **Wyoming:** Yellowstone NP.

CANADA

Alberta: Banff NP. **Manitoba:** Churchill; Riding Mt. NP. **Ontario:** Algonquin Provincial Pk.; Pt. Pelee NP. **Quebec:** Bonaventure Is.

SCIENTIFIC NAMES

Following are the scientific names of species illustrated in this book. The genus name is first; the species name follows. The numbers in heavy type indicate the pages where species are illustrated.

16 Lewis' Woodpecker: Melanerpes lewis
Pine Siskin: Carduelis pinus
18 Cyanocitta stelleri
19 Icteria virens
21 Gavia immer
22 Podilymbus podiceps
23 Ardea herodias
24 Butorides striatus
25 Bubulcus ibis
26 Cygnus columbianus
27 Branta canadensis
28 Anas platyrhynchos
29 Anas rubripes
30 Aix sponsa
31 Anas acuta
32 Aythya valisineria
33 Mergus merganser
34 Fulica americana
35 Charadrius vociferus
36 Gallinago gallinago
37 Tringa flavipes
38 Actitis macularia
39 Calidris minutilla
40 Larus argentatus
41 Sterna hirundo
42 Turkey: Cathartes aura
Black: Coragyps atratus
43 Pandion haliaetus
44 Haliaeetus leucocephalus
45 Accipiter cooperii
46 Buteo jamaicensis
47 Falco sparverius
48 Phasianus colchicus
49 Bonasa umbellus
50 Colinus virginianus

51 Columba livia
52 Zenaida macroura
53 Coccyzus americanus
54 Tyto alba
55 Bubo virginianus
56 Eastern: Otus asio
Western: Otus kennicottii
57 Chaetura pelagica
58 Caprimulgus vociferus
59 Chordeiles minor
60 Archilochus colubris
61 Ceryle alcyon
62 Melanerpes erythrocephalus
63 Colaptes auratus
64 Sphyrapicus varius
65 Picoides pubescens
66 Tyrannus tyrannus
67 Myiarchus crinitus
68 Sayornis phoebe
69 Empidonax minimus
70 Eremophila alpestris
71 Progne subis
72 Tachycineta bicolor
73 Hirundo rustica
74 Pica pica
75 Corvus brachyrhynchos
76 Cyanocitta cristata
77 Sitta carolinensis
78 Parus atricapillus
79 Parus bicolor
80 Certhia americana
81 Troglodytes aedon
82 Regulus calendula
83 Regulus satrapa
84 Polioptila caerulea

INDEX

Asterisks (*) denote pages on which birds are illustrated.

MEASURING SCALE (IN MILLIMETERS AND CENTIMETERS)

MEASURING SCALE (IN INCHES)

A B C D E F